A–Z OF CHELTENHAM

Places - People - History

David Elder

AMBERLEY

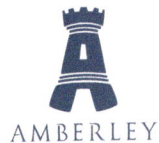

For Jane and Colin

First published 2019

Amberley Publishing
The Hill, Stroud, Gloucestershire, GL5 4EP
www.amberley-books.com

Copyright © David Elder, 2019

The right of David Elder to be identified as the Author of this work has been asserted in accordance with the Copyrights, Designs and Patents Act 1988.

ISBN 978 1 4456 8269 3 (print)
ISBN 978 1 4456 8270 9 (ebook)

All rights reserved. No part of this book may be reprinted or reproduced or utilised in any form or by any electronic, mechanical or other means, now known or hereafter invented, including photocopying and recording, or in any information storage or retrieval system, without the permission in writing from the Publishers.

British Library Cataloguing in Publication Data. A catalogue record for this book is available from the British Library.

Typesetting by Aura Technology and Software Services, India. Printed in Great Britain.

Contents

Introduction	5	Ichthyosaurus Communis	39
Aeroplane Field	6	Imperial Gardens	40
Alma House	7		
Fred Archer	8	Edward Jenner	41
		Jewish Burial Ground	42
Dorothea Beale	9	Brian Jones	43
Grace Billings	10		
Boer War Memorial	11	The Knapp	45
Brickyards	12	William Hill Knight	46
Cambray	13	Lamp Standards	47
Lewis Carroll	14	Lido	48
Caryatids	15		
Casino Place	16	William Charles Macready	50
River Chelt	17	Monson Avenue	51
Cheltenham Minster	18	Montpellier Gardens	51
Mrs Craik	19	Montpellier Rotunda	52
Samuel Whitfield Daukes	20		
Baron de Ferrières	21	Sir Charles Napier	54
Devil's Chimney	21	The Neptune Fountain	55
Dockem	22	Normal Terrace	56
George Dowty	23	Norwood Triangle	57
Eagle Tower	25	Old Bath Road	58
Everyman Theatre	26	Old Well Walk	59
		Outdoor Meeting Places	60
Lilian Faithfull	27		
Fancy Hall	28	Parabola Road	62
John Forbes	29	Richard Pate	63
		Penfold Pillar Boxes	64
GCHQ	30	Sir Thomas Phillipps	65
The Golden Valley	31	Pittville	66
Gordon Lamp	32	Post Offices	67
W. G. Grace	33	The Promenade	68
		Prestbury Park	69
High Street	34		
Gustav Holst	35	Quaker Burial Ground	70
George Holyoake	36	Quarries	71
Honeybourne Line	37	Queen's Hotel	72

A–Z of Cheltenham

Regent Arcade	73	William IV	87
Robert Burns Avenue	74	Dr Edward Wilson	87
		Winter Garden	89
Captain Henry Skillicorne	75		
St George's Place	76	(E)xmouth Arms	90
Town Hall	78	York Passage	91
Anthony Trollope	79		
Tuckwell Theatre	80	Zeppelin	92
		Zona Works	93
UCAS	82	Zoological Gardens	94
George Allen Underwood	83		
		Select Bibliography	95
Vittoria Walk	84	Acknowledgements	96
Hugo van Wadenoyen	85		
Well Place	86		

Introduction

Around 220 years ago the idea of compiling an A–Z guide to Cheltenham was difficult to entertain. John Leland's famous sixteenth-century description of the 'longe towne havynge a Market' reflected the fact that no urban extension had occurred beyond the single main street, also known as the Great Street or Cheltenham Street. Even by 1800, despite the tourism expansion following George III's endorsement of the spa twelve years earlier, the compiler of the town's first directory decided to depart from 'the usual alphabetical mode of publishing Directories' and simply walk along the north side of the High Street, incorporating any houses included in the side streets, and to do the same for the south side. However, such expedient methods proved impossible twenty years later: by 1821 the town's population had increased fourfold to 13,388, supplemented by a huge influx of visitors. Today a comprehensive study of the town's place names (see James Hodsdon's *An Historical Gazetteer of Cheltenham*) reveals the existence of around 3,000 toponyms, presenting a significant selection challenge to the compiler of this modest volume.

In this book I have focused on people and places with interesting, often lesser-known, narratives associated with the town's history and heritage. The stories of those who were born in Cheltenham or made their home here are as much part of the town's fabric as its streets and houses. They include actors, book collectors, builders, doctors, educationalists, explorers, military leaders, musicians, photographers, social reformers, sportsmen and writers. Their diversity alone is a reflection of the town's rich, fascinating history. Ordinary people are also centre stage. Who knows, for example, that, in addition to the Promenade's statue of Cheltenham-born Edward Wilson, the neighbouring statues of Neptune and the Boer War soldier were modelled on local people? Attention is also given to the makers of the town, not just the architects but the designers of its unique street furniture and its brick makers too.

The nature of the town is also revealed. Since its Regency heyday, for example, it has always been a place of entertainment, including, for instance, having one of the earliest puppet theatres. However, in this guide one aspect is most self-evident – the inevitability of change. Streets are constantly renamed, renumbered or even immortalised as 'ghost' names because they were only planned, never built. Equally, it is shown that the town's 'Post Office casts off its old quarters periodically as a crab casts his shell'. Of course, while an A–Z format implies a degree of completeness, such an aim is far from achievable, not least in a ninety-six-page book. Nevertheless, one of the pleasures of following this approach has been to uncover some of the people, places and events long forgotten or overlooked – from Henri Salmet's arrival at the Aeroplane Field (off Old Bath Road) in 1912 to the two rival schemes in the 1830s to establish zoological gardens in the town, a time when Brahman Bulls roared in The Park!

Aeroplane Field

Just over a century ago, one of the most unusual sites that could be imagined for a temporary airfield was located just below Leckhampton Hill, at the top end of Old Bath Road. Situated along the road's eastern edge, between the Pilford Road and Everest Road junctions was Rowlands Field, named after its owner. On 25 July 1912, as part of a tour aimed at popularising flying, then still in its infancy, Henri Salmet, the French chief instructor at the Blériot School at Hendon, landed his Blériot monoplane in what subsequently became known as 'the Aviation Ground' or 'the Aeroplane Field'. Earlier, possible alternative sites at the Racecourse or at Whaddon Farm were ruled out as being too small or inaccessible to the general public. However, after leaving Gloucester and negotiating some strong winds, Salmet landed safely, greeted by Cheltenham's mayor and a fervent crowd of around 2,500 onlookers. Following a short exhibition flight, Salmet departed for Cirencester. After ascending above Leckhampton Hill, he headed over Charlton Kings, Pittville, the High Street, Lansdown, and Hatherley Road before turning south, eventually rising to a height of 3,000 feet within 45 minutes. This was only the second time Cheltonians might have seen an aeroplane, the first being witnessed by some in

The aviators who flew to Cheltenham on 23 October 1913.

A

October 1911. Further opportunities arose in 1913 when three more aviation events were held in the field, including on 23 October when three Old Cheltonian army aviators flew from the Netheravon Flying School to attend the wedding of a college friend in Cheltenham. Following the outbreak of the First World War the field was never used again for flying, and today is largely a residential area.

Alma House

Unusual in a place hailed as the most complete Regency town is Alma House (in Rodney Road), a stunning masterpiece of Arts and Crafts design! At first glance it appears as one of many Regency villas, but the conservatory extension on the south-facing wall gives a clue from the outside of a 'secret' interior. Built in the 1830s, and originally known as Rodney Villa, it was renamed Alma House in celebration of Britain's victory at the 1854 Crimean War battle. In 1905 the then owner, dentist George Peake, decided to refurbish the villa. Peake had become interested in the Arts and Crafts and art nouveau movements whose practitioners offered customers a more pared down look than that of often cluttered Victorian homes all over Britain. Peake commissioned a complete decorative scheme from Scottish architect-cum-designer George Walton, who had forged a reputation in Glasgow designing (including in collaboration with his friend Charles Rennie Mackintosh) Miss Cranston's The Willow Tearooms. Implementation of Walton's designs was entrusted to leading Cheltenham firm H. H. Martyn & Co. and the finished scheme – which combines aspects of Glasgow School, Arts and Crafts movement and art nouveau styles – featured in the 1907 yearbook of the prestigious *Studio* magazine.

Below left: Alma House.

Below right: Door leading to the conservatory.

A–Z of Cheltenham

Fred Archer

One of the most successful jockeys of all time, Frederick James Archer (1857–86) was born in Cheltenham at St George's Cottage (now No. 43 St George's Place), today marked by a commemorative plaque. From the age of two, he grew up at the King's Arms in Prestbury where his father, a steeplechase rider who won the Grand National in 1858, had retired to become landlord. From the age of eleven he was apprenticed for five years to a leading Newmarket trainer, a year later winning his first race when weighing just 4 stone 11 pounds. In a remarkable career he rode 2,748 winners from 8,084 starts, achieving the accolade of champion jockey of England by the age of seventeen, a position he held for thirteen consecutive years from 1874 to 1886. Although regularly visiting his family in Prestbury, where he continued to ride with the Cotswold Hunt, Archer made Newmarket his home. Unfortunately, his worldwide fame came at a significant cost to his health. An unusually tall (1.74 metres) jockey, Archer was forced to follow a strict diet and take purgatives and Turkish baths to keep his weight under control. This, coupled with gambling problems and the tragedies of losing his son at birth and then his wife, ten months later, led him into a spiral of deep depression. Suffering also from typhoid, he shot himself with a revolver, kept to protect his family, following a spate of burglaries in Newmarket.

Archer riding the racehorse Ormonde, by John Cameron, 1889.

Dorothea Beale

Today, while Cheltenham is well known as a centre for education, its contribution to advances in educational reform deserve wider appreciation. Without doubt, its greatest pioneer was Dorothea Beale (1831–1906), the longest-serving principal of Cheltenham Ladies' College. It was through Miss Beale that the Ladies' College was transformed, placing as much emphasis on the process of learning, and thereby encouraging independent thinking, as on achieving high levels of educational attainment. During her forty-eight years' tenure as principal, Miss Beale introduced many reforms, several of which were considered radical at the time. Of particular significance was her broadening of the curriculum to include science, mathematics

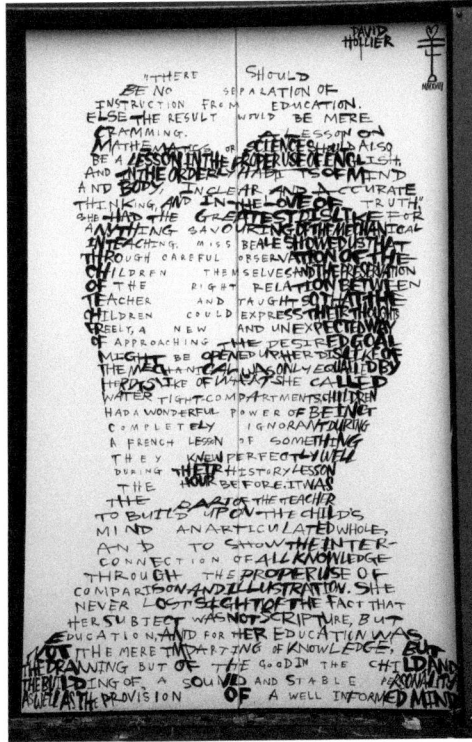

Dorothea Beale, by David Hollier (2018), which uses biographical text about her.

and classics, the introduction of physical education, and the establishment of a teacher-training department, St Hilda's College. Later amalgamated with St Hilda's Hall, Oxford (also established by Miss Beale), where it became one of the first women's colleges, the original St Hilda's was established as an adjunct to the Ladies' College in Western Road, where it is now used as a boarding house.

Grace Billings

One of Cheltenham's least-known women pioneers, who became a highly respected doctor in what was then a traditionally male occupation, was Grace Billings, née Stewart (1872–1957). Initially living at Ariel Lodge (no longer in existence but marked by a modern housing development on Ariel Lodge Road), Grace Billings underwent medical training in London, Edinburgh and Newcastle. Returning to Cheltenham in 1899, she became the first woman in Gloucestershire to set up a medical practice, and possibly even the first woman to set up in Britain as a general practitioner. Although facing much prejudice at the time, and not always taken seriously, she gained respect locally by giving lectures and training courses, and getting involved in professional circles. As the only woman among forty-one doctors within the town, she stood out,

Dr Billings (front row, centre) as medical superintendent of St Martin's Hospital.

especially when smoking after-dinner cigars with the men! During the First World War she contributed by acting as medical superintendent of St Martin's Hospital, established in a boarding house at Cheltenham Ladies' College to care for sick or wounded soldiers. Today, a blue plaque records her first medical practice at No. 3 Pittville Parade (now No. 6 Evesham Road).

Boer War Memorial

A plan for a memorial to commemorate the Cheltenham men who served in the Second Boer War (1899–1902) originally proposed mural tablets to be placed in the public library. Then, in 1904, a design by Charles Letheren for a tablet in bronze and hammered copper was selected by the town council. The 6-foot-square tablet, comprising the borough crest and the roots, trunk and foliage of an oak tree, was to be placed in the Town Hall lobby. However, the legality of using public funds for this purpose was raised, and the focus changed to raising the necessary funds by public subscription. At length, the design for a 7-foot-high bronze statue by Ambrose Neale of the local firm of R. L. Boulton, was accepted. Boulton had previously produced a well-regarded Boer War statue (now at the Edward Brooks Barracks, Shippon) for the 1st Battalion Oxfordshire Light Infantry. For the design of the Cheltenham statue, Neale, who was educated at Cheltenham Grammar School, modelled some of

Boer War Memorial, 1907.

A–Z of Cheltenham

the details of the figure, that of a private soldier, standing at ease in reflective mood with arms reversed, from a veteran whose name is commemorated on the Portland stone pedestal below. Positioned at the south end of the Promenade Long Garden, it was unveiled on 7 July 1907 by General Sir Ian Hamilton, who spoke passionately about the sixty men who 'died by the banks of the swift Tugela; ... fell in the treacherous ravines and on the rocky kopjes of the high veldt; [and] ... are buried here and there in desolate places among the haroo bushes of the Cape'. The mayor commented that one in five of those who perished had been mentioned in despatches 'for their gallantry and useful work' and that nearly 2,000 officers and men, who had taken part in the war, could be considered 'to belong to Cheltenham' through residency or close relationships. Another impressive memorial, built c. 1902, that also commemorates the war, is located at the entrance to Cheltenham College.

Brickyards

The ready availability of Lias clay and local sand provided Cheltenham with the raw materials to manufacture the bricks used to build the original spa town. During the nineteenth century brickyards were established in Portland Street, Coltham Field (near Haywards Road), Leckhampton, Battledown, Alstone, and Lower Pilley. Brick making was so fundamental to Cheltenham's building tradition that some brickyard owners claimed that the industry was established by King Alfred the Great. Frederick Thackwell established his brickyard in the late 1830s close to the site of the future Leckhampton railway station. By 1872 it was producing 420,000 clamp-fired bricks annually. Thackwell's yard struggled as sand needed to be transported over a distance of 3 miles, and the finished bricks delivered into the town via a toll gate. When Thackwell died in 1876, the business was promoted as a pottery, eventually trading as Cotswold Potteries Ltd until it ceased in 1912. It had also suffered from growing competition from the Battledown yard, which dominated the local market during the twentieth century, closing only in 1971 as the town's last brick-making business.

Thackwell Brick.

C

Cambray

The Cambray name, known since the 1560s, and originally given to a meadow (seen as 'Canbry meade' in 1605) south of High Street, reputedly derived from a local family who came from Cambrai in France. When it was developed in the early nineteenth century using funding from a tontine scheme, Cambray Place (the section between Bath Street and High Street originally called Cambray Street) attracted professional people. Among these was a physician living at No. 30, whose son, Gilbert Jessop, became a famous cricketer. Renowned as a hard-hitting batsman, Jessop scored over 26,500 runs in 569 test matches. Nicknamed 'The Croucher' because of his hunched stance at the crease, he also holds the record for the fastest test century by an England batsman, scoring 100 off 76 balls in less than an hour against Australia in 1902. Jessop also played football for Cheltenham Town. In 1824 the poet Elizabeth Barrett Browning visited No. 8 where some of her relatives, the Graham-Clarkes, lived. In 1854 Cheltenham Ladies' College opened its doors for the first time at Cambray House, a site now occupied by Cambray Court flats. In 1873 it transferred to its current purpose-built accommodation in Bayshill. Interestingly, there is also a Cambray Parade marked prominently on the 1825 town map. However, this ambitious scheme to build 200 houses failed without a brick being laid. Its only contribution was to create a 'ghost' name!

Cambray Place looking south. Cambray House is just visible above the handcart.

A–Z of Cheltenham

Lewis Carroll

Charles Dodgson (1832–98), better known as Lewis Carroll, made a memorable visit to Cheltenham in 1863. Staying at the Belle Vue Hotel (now Cedar House flats), London Road, he visited the Liddell family. Alice Liddell, who originally inspired Carroll to write *Alice's Adventures in Wonderland* (1865), was staying at her grandparents' house, Hetton Lawn, Cudnall Street, in Charlton Kings. During his visit Carroll saw the ornate mirror at Hetton Lawn which, it is believed, later inspired him to write *Through the Looking Glass* (1871). Today the mirror, with its figures of a shepherd, shepherdess, birds and nests, is located on the first-floor landing of the house, but when their granddaughter Alice stayed at the house it was situated above the fireplace in the drawing room. It reflected the garden through the tall windows, suggesting you could enter through it into a different world.

It is also thought that the visit provided further inspiration for Carroll. When he took Alice and her two sisters for a walk on Leckhampton Hill, they looked down on the Severn Vale countryside, which appeared, as described in *Wonderland*, 'marked out just like a giant chess board'. Also accompanying them on the walk was Miss Prickett, the children's governess who, according to Carroll, was the prototype for the Red Queen, 'the concentrated essence of all governesses!' Finally, in the evening, Carroll, who was interested in magic, took the girls to the Assembly Rooms (whose site on the High Street is now occupied by Lloyds Bank) to see Herr Döbler, a famous Viennese magician. It is thought that this provided Carroll with further inspiration for *Alice's*

The mirror thought to have inspired *Through the Looking Glass*.

Adventures in Wonderland. One of the illusions in the show was called Professor Pepper's Ghost, which involved making objects appear and disappear through the use of mirrors and lighting. Inspired by this, Carroll later added the 'Pig and Pepper' chapter to his book, which included the famous description of the Cheshire Cat who 'vanished quite slowly beginning with the end of the tail and ending with the grin'.

Caryatids

Among the distinctive features in Montpellier Walk are the thirty-two armless white caryatid figures, some with a left and some a right knee bent forward, which provide support to the shop lintels. Based on the design of the caryatids supporting the Erechtheion temple's portico on the Athenian Acropolis, it is thought that three original terracotta figures were brought back from London by Pearson Thompson, perhaps inspired by sculptor J. F. C. Rossi's use of caryatid columns at St Pancras Church in 1819. The others were copied in stone by local craftsmen, James Brown (1803–71) and his son William (1828–1926), and two were recently reproduced in concrete. James Brown contributed to the building or embellishment of many of Cheltenham's principal buildings during the first half of the nineteenth century, including Pittville Pump Room, Cheltenham College and its chapel, Christ Church, St Luke's Church, and Salem Chapel. The origin of the caryatids' use appears to derive from an ancient Greek victory over the Carian people who had sided with the Greeks' enemies. Following the conquest, the Greeks

Caryatid, Montpellier Walk.

enslaved the Carian women and, to further perpetuate the Carians' disgrace, used their figures as architectural columns in public buildings. Interestingly, remarkably similar versions of the Cheltenham designs are also present in Toulouse, suggesting the Virebent manufactory, Toulouse, may be the source of our caryatids.

Casino Place

Named after Casino House, advertised in 1824 as a 'very elegant villa with 14 rooms', Casino Place is a good example of one of the unobtrusive lanes that serviced some of the town's grandest dwellings. Originally built for William Whitehead, Casino House had a richly decorated interior, which included a geometrical staircase built of Bath stone and an entrance hall with marble-inset floors. By 1830 it had become a boys' school run by William Childe and, a year later, the venue for Mrs Wells's 'Seminary for Young Ladies', previously located at Castleton House (now Courtfield) in Charlton Kings, where the 'Pestalozzian Method of Object Lessons', based on the child-centred approaches promoted by Swiss educational reformer Johann Heinrich Pestalozzi, was taught. On 24 December 1833 the house celebrated the marriage between the widow Dorothea Wells and George Heywood, a city broker. However, eight months later the *Cheltenham Chronicle* was to report the bigamy trial of Heywood who was later sent to Newgate Prison for six months for having previously married a woman in Bristol. By 1878 Casino House had become a boys' school, transferred from neighbouring Painswick Lawn House, and was known as Haldon House. In the 1930s it was demolished to build Nos 2–12 Painswick Road. Today, Casino House is recalled through the surviving perimeter brick wall in Casino Place and a stone pier on the corner of St James's Place. It is also recalled through Haldon (or Holden's) Cottage in Casino Place, probably its only remaining outbuilding. By 1926 Casino Place accommodated seventeen houses, previously home to low-paid workers, including farm labourers, domestic servants, carters, fly drivers, gardeners and dressmakers. Ten years later ten of the cottages were demolished as part of a slum-clearance programme.

Casino House.

River Chelt

Rising in the Cotswolds above Dowdeswell, the Chelt flows north-west through Cheltenham and, around 11 miles later, enters the River Severn at Wainlodes Hill. Its earliest name, recorded in the twelfth century as Alre or Arle (meaning 'alder-tree'), probably indicated that alders grew along it. The river gave its name to the borough's western tithing, Arle, the oldest place name in the Cheltenham area. While the name Chelt was first used c. 1540, probably a back-formation of the town's name, the river was also called Awbrook or Hawbrook and the Incham during the sixteenth and seventeenth centuries. Although a small river, which today for much of its course through the town centre is hidden from view, it has played a significant part in Cheltenham's history. In medieval times the settlement that ranged along its single main street (later the High Street) ran parallel to the river. The river also fuelled the town's early economy through the medieval mills sited at Sandford, Cambray, Arle, Alstone and, possibly, Cudnall. Here waterfalls powered the mill wheels as water cascaded down from hard outcrops of clayey limestone. Enclosures of pasture also bordered the river. During much of the seventeenth century the Chelt's banks were one of the places used to grow the town's crops of tobacco, declared illegal from 1619. The river was the scene of a minor skirmish during the English Civil War when Parliamentary forces engaged with Royalist troops on 4 September 1643 after advancing towards the Chelt through Prestbury from Cleeve Hill. The river once provided the location for a cold bath, with facilities for warm bathing too. Located not far from what is now the Bayshill Inn, this was run by a Miss Stapleton from 1763 and offered medicinal baths, sometimes recommended by physicians as a supplement to drinking the waters. This bath became disused by 1783 while other bathing establishments were later set up in the High Street and in Bath Road. As the town centre became more developed during the 1820s and 1830s, the river became culverted and covered over along this stretch of its course. In contrast, some residents were keen to make the river a more prominent feature. Colonel Riddell, who owned Wellington Mansion (now demolished), changed the course of the river near Wellington Street so that it flowed through the middle of his garden, siting an oak tree on the river bank and, later, an obelisk (demolished 1862) to commemorate the Duke of Wellington.

River Chelt at Spring Bottom, Charlton Kings.

Although a small river, visitors sometimes mistakenly dismiss the Chelt as just a stream. The American essayist Washington Irving recalled in 1820 that, while returning from a walk to the spas, he inquired about the name of 'that pretty brook'. A resident replied that it was not a brook but the river Chelt, after which Irving half-expected to see the stream 'avenge the affront'! Today, residents are respectful of the river's strength. The devastating floods it caused in 2007 were estimated to have cost the borough council around £8.8 million. Throughout history the Chelt has been much given to flooding. As a short, steep river, which itself is served by several tributaries, it reacts to heavy rain quickly. A typical occurrence of the river bursting its banks was reported in the *Cheltenham Examiner* on 26 July 1855: 'in a very few minutes the whole of the houses from the Bath-road to Alstone, and occupying a belt of some three hundred yards in width, had their basements flooded from three to four feet in depth'. Today, a flood alleviation scheme has been designed to protect the town.

Cheltenham Minster

Originally called St Mary's Church, Cheltenham Minster is the town's oldest building, some of its arches dating from *c.* 1170. The building possibly replaced a Saxon church erected four centuries earlier. Its rose window features fourteenth-century tracery and Victorian glass. It also contains several interesting memorials, including to Henry Skillicorne, the developer of the spa, and Hannah Forty, one of the spa pumpers. In the churchyard, on the north-east side, are the remains of a fourteenth-century preaching cross from which John Wesley (1703–91) once preached. However, the townsfolk left a poor impression on him. During his visit on 8 May 1744 he recorded, 'I preached [at Cheltenham] on, "By grace are ye saved through faith," to a company who seemed to understand just as much of the matter, as if I had been talking Greek.' His final visit to Cheltenham in 1784 did not fare much better. On this occasion he recorded that 'I preached at noon to half a houseful of hearers, most of them cold and dead enough.' The churchyard also includes the well-known tombstone commemorating John Higgs

St Mary's Church (from *Cheltenham and its Neighbourhood, c.* 1871).

who died in 1825. The amusing epitaph reads: 'Here lies John Higgs / a famous man for killing pigs / for killing pigs was his delight / both morning, afternoon and night / both heats and colds he did endure / which no Physician could e'er cure, / his knife is laid, his work is done, / hope to heaven his soul is gone.' On the south side of the churchyard, set in the path, there are brass measuring marks, approximately 7 centimetres in length, which were once used by nearby market traders to check the measurements of rope and cloth.

Mrs Craik

One of the authors to portray Cheltenham through the disguise of a fictitious place was Dinah Craik (née Mulock, 1826–87). She gained inspiration from a visit in 1852–53, when she stayed at Detmore (London Road, Charlton Kings), family home of the poet Sydney Dobell. She named the town Coltham, taking this from Coltham Lane (now Hales Road) which formed part of the Cheltenham–Charlton Kings boundary, and used it as the setting for the early scenes of her most popular novel, *John Halifax, Gentleman* (1856). Coltham was described as a place which 'patronized by royalty, rivalled even Bath in its fashion and folly'. Detmore itself appears in the novel as a house called Longfield, named after Longfield Cottage, Stoke-on-Trent where the author was born: 'Longfield! happy Longfield! Little nest of love, and joy, and peace – where the children grew up, and we grew old ... It had one parlour, three decent bedrooms, kitchen and out-houses.'

One memorable scene in the novel involves two of the main characters, who visit the 'Coffee-house yard' theatre to see Mrs Siddons act. They catch a glimpse of her in a sedan en route to the theatre. Here, Mrs Craik drew on real events and places. Coffee House Yard was Cheltenham's first recorded theatre. Established in 1758 in a converted malthouse, the site is now occupied by part of Pittville Street. Sarah Siddons (1755–1831) acted there in 1774 where her acting prowess was recognised at an early age.

Detmore today, which featured as Longfield in Mrs Craik's novel.

Samuel Whitfield Daukes

One of the most respected architects who contributed greatly to Cheltenham's built environment was Samuel Whitfield Daukes (1811–80). Based in Gloucester and London, he has been described as a 'convinced eclecticist' who was adept at working with all the fashionable styles of the day. This was well illustrated in his Cheltenham work, which ranges from the Greek Revival and Italianate architecture he produced when designing villas for the Park Estate from the late 1830s, to the Norman Revival he used for St Peter's Church in 1846–49, and the Gothic Revival for St Paul's College in 1848. Other fine examples of his work can be found in the Lansdown railway station, built in 1840 originally with an impressive portico unfortunately demolished in 1961, the houses and shops at Nos 1–19, Montpellier Street constructed c. 1844–51, the Italianate-designed Lypiatt Terrace (1847), and Francis Close Hall (1848–50). Despite Daukes's ability to work across many different styles, in later life he failed, or possibly did not choose, to embrace the new styles favoured during the High Victorian period. Although he continued work in the Midlands, his business started to decline in the 1860s.

Lypiatt Terrace, 1910.

D

Portrait of Baron de Ferrières in Cheltenham Masonic Hall.

Baron de Ferrières

One of the town's great benefactors, the larger-than-life Baron Charles Conrad Adolphus du Bois de Ferrières (1823–1908) was the grandson of a Napoleonic general. Born in Utrecht, he came to Cheltenham with his family in 1860, eventually living at Bays Hill House (its site now occupied by Sidney Lodge) where George III stayed during his visit in 1788. Forty years later he was made a freeman of the town, having been active in Cheltenham public life, including as its second mayor in 1877–78, and its Liberal MP in 1880–85. A leading Freemason, his obituary notice stated that there was 'scarcely a society or charitable institution in the town that [had] not benefited from his support'. Of particular note was his donation in 1898 of forty-three paintings from his father's collection of seventeenth-century Dutch masters and nineteenth-century Belgian work, many on display in the Friends' Gallery at The Wilson, together with £1,000 towards establishing the town's art gallery. De Ferrieres Walk, off Marsland Road, Hester's Way, was named after him in 1953.

Devil's Chimney

One of the instantly recognisable sights commonly used to portray Cheltenham since the early nineteenth century, the Devil's Chimney has acted as a sentinel overlooking the town

Above left: The Devil's Chimney, lithograph by Henry Lamb, *c.* 1825.

Above right: Looking towards Cheltenham from the Devil's Chimney.

from the slopes of Leckhampton Hill. Theories about its true origin included speculation by eminent geologist Sydney Savory Buckman that it was formed through natural differential erosion. However, it is commonly accepted, as evidenced by lithographs from the 1820s, that it was fashioned into shape by quarrymen after the construction of a tramroad incline (the county's first goods railroad), left a stack of limestone rock jutting out from the face of the hill. So-named from at least 1803, when Ruff's *History of Cheltenham* curiously described it, 'Built by the devil, as say the vulgar. It was no doubt built by shepherds in the frolic of an idle hour'; since then it has perhaps been a remarkable publicity stunt or, at least, motif for the town. In *c.* 1920 it was the subject of a poignant poem by Ivor Gurney who imagined that the 'Watcher of west England' had fallen down 'like a stick or a tree'. In 1926, following earth tremors, Gurney's fears were nearly realised when large cracks appeared on the rock. Its integrity was further jeopardised by the popularity of scaling its heights, culminating in a 1959 achievement when thirteen rock climbers from Gloucestershire Mountaineering Club succeeded in squeezing themselves simultaneously onto the summit. In the mid-1980s the council spent £20,000 strengthening the structure, and climbing the rock is now banned.

Dockem

Also referred to as Dockum, or Dockham, and particularly used with the prefix 'Lower', Dockem is the unofficial name for the lower end of the town. Doubt surrounds both its origin and precise location, some claiming that it refers to the area between Henrietta

Lower High Street.

Street and Gloucester Road, others suggesting it extends west to incorporate the parish of St Peter's. Perhaps the earliest documented reference comes from a comic song called 'The Dandy Flyman of Lower Dockem', sung by 'Jim Crow' in 1835. The name has usually been associated with a poor reputation. In 1863 Cheltenham's historian John Goding described it as a place where 'people of respect are afraid to live … Persons are stoned and pelted with mud … [and where] one or two have lost their lives'. This would account for one theory that the name derived from the frequency with which Dockem residents would appear in the police court dock. Other possibilities include that it derived from nearby Gloucester, which has a Dockham Lane, or from boggy land where docks grew. It may even have been inspired by the projected Cheltenham dock terminus of the Coombe Hill canal. Whatever the truth, the name has added 'colour' to the local geography and has not always carried stigma. In 1940, for example, a reader of the *Cheltenham Chronicle* wrote to the editor, telling of 'one esteemed citizen who quite often on Sunday mornings prefers a walk down Lower High-street to Tewkesbury-road bridge to going to church although, be it said, he is a good Churchman'.

George Dowty

It was at No. 10 Lansdown Terrace Lane that the aeronautical engineer Sir George Dowty (1901–75) set up a workshop, from which the future Dowty Group of Companies grew. Interested in engineering from an early age after his brother-in-law gave him a model steam engine, Dowty went on to work for various engineering firms before joining the Gloster Aircraft Company (GAC) in 1924. While working there he invented an internally sprung landing wheel, which led to an order for six being placed in 1931 by the Japanese Kawasaki Aircraft Company. Although GAC was unable to meet the order, Dowty set up his own company, Aircraft Components Ltd, to make them himself. Working initially from the Lansdown premises, a rented mews loft above a wheelwright's, apart from the potential fire risk from wood shavings below, Dowty's team also had to contend with a petrol store next door. After completing the Kawasaki order in September 1931, the company moved to larger premises in Grosvenor Place. Further expansion followed and, by 1934, the forty-five-strong company had established offices in Bath Street. To cope with increasing orders Dowty bought Arle Court (now Manor by the Lake) in 1935 where the 100-acre site could accommodate workshops and other facilities.

From here, the company supplied nearly all the hydraulic systems, undercarriage units, tail wheels, electrical instruments and warning devices used by British aircraft during the Second World War, including the Allies' first jet aircraft, the Gloster Whittle E28/39, and the first jet fighter to see action, the Gloster Meteor. By the time George Dowty was given the Freedom of the Borough in 1955 his worldwide group of twenty-five companies was the largest manufacturer of aircraft equipment in Europe.

Dowty is also remembered as a generous benefactor, donating £2,000 (instead of buying a new Rolls-Royce) to help establish a home for the elderly in the former boys' orphanage (now flats) in St Margaret's Road which, during its sixty-years' existence as a care home from 1958, was known as Dowty House.

Above: Sir George Dowty.

Left: No. 10 Lansdown Terrace Lane, where Dowty set up his workshop (inset).

E

Eagle Tower

The most conspicuous and controversial of all Cheltenham's buildings is the 161-foot, thirteen-storey-high Eagle Tower building, which originally served as the administrative head office and computer centre for Eagle Star Insurance. Opened in 1968 at a cost of £1.7 million as part of the office decentralisation policy of the mid-1960s, it has dominated the town's skyline ever since. When Old Cheltonian film director and actor Lindsay Anderson used Cheltenham College as the backdrop for the school scenes in the film *If* (1968), one of the difficulties he identified during filming was how to exclude from view the neighbouring tower block. Its construction required the demolition of a hotel and two Regency villas in Montpellier Parade, including Westal, family home of Antarctic explorer Edward Wilson who resided there from 1874. However, a much greater proportion of the town's heritage might have been lost but for successful opposition to a more radical local council proposal in 1966 to redevelop the town's centre. Although the building, designed by Stone, Toms and Partners, has been

Eagle Tower.

described variously as 'hideous and ill-conceived' and a 'graceless bulk' which is totally out of scale within its immediate vicinity, it also has its admirers and there is no doubt that the architects achieved part of their aim which was to signal the dawn of a new era. Today, the building serves a number of small and medium-sized businesses.

Everyman Theatre

The Everyman Theatre, originally styled The New Theatre and Opera House when it opened in 1891, is the oldest surviving example of the work of Frank Matcham, one of the country's great theatre architects. His two hundred works include London's Palladium and Coliseum. One of the hallmarks of his innovative design was the use of steel cantilevers to support balconies. This enabled increased audience capacity and avoided the spoiling of sightlines by pillars. The building's restrained decoration on its façade contrasts with some glittering splendour in its interior. Particularly noteworthy is the flat ceiling which, via a clever optical illusion, creates the impression of being dome shaped.

Cheltenham's long theatrical tradition dates back to the mid-eighteenth century when a converted malthouse and stables (site near Pittville Street) provided a venue for some of the country's most accomplished actors of the day, including Sarah Siddons and her brother John Kemble. This theatre was renamed the Theatre Royal following King George III's visit to Cheltenham in 1788. About a century later, a group of enterprising local citizens was prompted to commission the building of a new theatre after another venue (now occupied by the Princess Hall) was acquired by Cheltenham Ladies' College. The new theatre opened with a performance by Lillie Langtry on 1 October 1891.

During the first half of the twentieth century the theatre prospered, attracting famous actors such as Laurence Olivier and Charlie Chaplin. However, in 1959 the increasing popularity of television threatened its closure. To revive its fortunes, in 1960 it was relaunched as the Everyman following refurbishment and the creation of a new repertory company. Since then the theatre has undergone further restoration, increasing success through broadening its range of activities in keeping with the 'Everyman' brand. Today, performances are given in its 700-seat main auditorium or 60-seat Studio Theatre, previously known as The Richardson after the Cheltenham-born actor Ralph Richardson.

The Everyman Theatre.

Lilian Faithfull

One of the names synonymous with social care in Cheltenham is Lilian Faithfull (1865–1952). Remembered as someone who cared deeply about the welfare of her students during her 1907–22 tenure as principal of the Ladies' College, she was fondly portrayed as Miss Helen Butterfield in Margaret Kennedy's novel *The Constant Nymph* (1924), who 'saw the girls if anybody had died' and gave talks on topics such as fortitude and friendship. While at college she was also one of the first women magistrates to be appointed in England when she became a Cheltenham JP in 1920. Continuing to work during her retirement well into her eighties, she turned her attention to the care of the elderly at the end of the Second World War. Given the severe housing shortages at the time, she recognised that a practical solution was required to cater adequately for the needs of the elderly. In 1946 she set up the Cheltenham Old Peoples' Housing Society Ltd,

Lilian Faithfull.

a non-profit-making charity. Today branded as Lilian Faithfull Care, the charity runs four residential care homes in Cheltenham, in Fiddlers Green Lane and at Astell House (in Overton Park Road), St Faith's (in Malvern Road), and Faithfull House (in Suffolk Square). Lilian Faithfull died in Faithfull House in 1952, a Civic Society plaque recording that the residential home opened in October 1951. She is buried in the town cemetery.

Fancy Hall

Fancy Hall, now Nos 2–4 Montpellier Parade, home of the New Club, gained some notoriety in 1827 as the origin of an influential legal case, quoted in divorce courts for decades afterwards. The case of Hamerton v Hamerton originally entered in the Consistory Court in Gloucester, lasted over two years, and was brought to appeal at the Court of Chancery. Major William Meadows Hamerton brought the case against his wife, Isabella Frances, née Romer. The couple, then resident at Fancy Hall, had arrived in Cheltenham in 1825. While living there Isabella began an adulterous relationship with John Bushe Esq., the eldest son of the Lord Chief Justice of Ireland, who lived with his wife, Lady Louisa, at No. 2 Oxford Parade (No. 46 London Road). He was also a confidant of the notorious Colonel Willam Fitzhardinge Berkeley. Isabella first became acquainted with Bushe at a ball she gave in January 1826, one witness claiming that the couple had kissed on the stairs at that ball.

Clandestine meeting places included Colonel Crowder's at No. 6 St Margaret's Terrace, Colonel Ollney's at The Pavilion (site now Wetherspoons, Bath Road) and at Malcolm Ghur (now known as Pillar House, Bath Road). In February Major Hamerton, perhaps suspecting that Bushe was in pursuit of his wife, asked Isabella to break off all acquaintance with him. However, the clandestine meetings continued for more than a

The Hall, 1901 (formerly called Fancy Hall).

year. On 25 March 1827 Major Hamerton received an anonymous letter informing him of his wife's indiscretions. He became certain that adultery had been committed after discovering incriminating letters from Bushe in Isabella's trinket box. A separation immediately took place: Major and Mrs Hamerton left Fancy Hall in a fly, and the major returned alone. He never saw her again. Although commencing an Action at Law against John Bushe for Criminal Conversation with his wife, it was not possible to serve a writ as Bushe left Cheltenham for France the next day. Isabella joined him in Paris and they continued their adulterous relationship there and later in Switzerland. In December 1830 Major Hamerton obtained £1,000 damages against John Bushe, who had previously admitted his dishonourable conduct to the Sheriff's Court.

John Forbes

One of the most skilled local architects who, for various reasons, was unable to fulfil his promising early career was John Forbes (c. 1790). Forbes's unquestionable talent can still be appreciated in his design of Pittville Pump Room, the layout of the Pittville Estate, St Paul's Church and various other buildings, including the Beehive pub in Montpellier. A series of unfortunate events when he dabbled as a building speculator between the late 1820s and early 1830s led him into debt and then, following a case of forgery, into imprisonment for two years. Sadly, nothing more was heard of Forbes from about 1838, but his legacy of fine examples of neoclassical architecture is a tangible reminder of his considerable talent.

Pittville Pump Room, designed by John Forbes.

GCHQ

Cheltenham is today well known as the home of Government Communications Headquarters (GCHQ), one of the three UK Intelligence and Security Agencies that work alongside the Security Service (MI5) and the Secret Intelligence Service (MI6). Its functions were first avowed on 12 May 1983 following the trial of Geoffrey Prime, a GCHQ linguist who had been spying for the Russians. Further publicity was aroused in 1984 when trade unions were banned at GCHQ 'in the interests of national security'. Today, employing over 6,000 people, its intelligence is used to counter the threats posed particularly from terrorism and serious crime and to support UK law enforcement and military operations. Its cyber-security function was expanded in 2016 by the creation of the National Cyber Security Centre (NCSC), a key part of the UK's defence against cyberattacks.

Its main building, widely known as the 'Doughnut', was completed in 2003 and officially opened by HM the Queen on 24 March 2004. Its architecture received many accolades, including one describing it as 'a superbly designed and finished building ... perfectly fitting GCHQ's post Cold War aspiration to be flexible and able to respond to change rapidly, 24 hours a day'. The scale of the building is best appreciated from the air. Its roof comprises over 11,000 square metres of aluminium, while its central courtyard is big enough to accommodate the Royal Albert Hall.

GCHQ's association with Cheltenham began in 1950 when staff were transferred from Eastcote under a government dispersal scheme. News that it was a Foreign Office department and not a 'less desirable' branch of the civil service was greeted with a sigh of relief by the town's deputy mayor. Initially, GCHQ set up a small set of offices in Clarence Street to manage the move from Eastcote. Thereafter, it occupied two sites, at Benhall Farm and Oakley, sites used by the US Army during the Second World War. To accommodate the influx of new residents the council built new housing stock, mostly in the Hester's Way area. 'Managerial' houses were also built to accommodate some of the senior staff in Ledmore Road, Charlton Kings, and Oldfield Crescent in St Marks. Approaching the needs of the twenty-first century, however, a new building was needed, particularly to foster a more collaborative working environment. As an intelligence and security agency, GCHQ depends on creating innovative solutions

Above: Aerial view showing GCHQ's 'doughnut' shape.

Right: The central 'street' during a family day event.

to challenging problems. In view of this, a circular design, incorporating open plan offices with a wide 'street' running between them, was conceived to facilitate effective knowledge sharing. GCHQ remains one of the area's largest employers, and its presence has encouraged other nearby high-tech industries. It also adds a touch of mystery and intrigue to Cheltenham and an international renown, a far cry from its small market town origins.

The Golden Valley

Today, well known in the context of the Golden Valley Bypass, which links Cheltenham and Gloucester along the A40, the name Golden Valley referred *c.* 1813 to the area west of the former Pheasant Inn on the B4063, the old road to Gloucester, then called the Golden Valley Lane. Its name is still associated locally with the hotel near the Arle Court roundabout, formerly the Golden Valley Hotel, which came to fame in 1981–84 as the *Crossroads* motel in the long-running ITV soap opera. While the name conjures up a scene of tranquillity, in February 1876 an odd dispute occurred within the area that led to the resignation of an Anglican Church minister and the demolition of the Golden Valley Chapel, known unofficially as 'the Little Church in the Valley'. Established in 1861 by Packer Butt, the owner of Arle Court (now Manor by the Lake), the small wooden church was officially known as St Peter's in the Valley, and also as Arle Court Church. It appears that Butt and his sister-in-law resented what they perceived as interference by Revd Alfred Hall. While the congregation sympathised with their minister's stance, Butt refused to compromise. Despite attempts made to purchase the church from Butt, according to the *Cheltenham Mercury* the excitement became so great 'that the offending couple were made the "butts" for wordy abuse

Former chapel, on which site the earlier Golden Valley chapel was demolished.

and the more forcible arguments of stones and dirt' to the extent that they had to be rescued by a policeman. 'Early next morning', it continued, 'Mr Butt revenged himself upon his irate neighbours by engaging a gang of labourers from Cheltenham to demolish the Church'. The biased reporter concluded that it was only a question of 'whether the act was directed by a bad-man or a mad-man!' Although the true cause of the dispute was never categorically revealed, it is certain that it involved what Revd Hall described was an 'interference in church matters by a member of Mr Butt's household'. One theory points to Butt's eldest son, William, who was a strong advocate of the Church of England Oxford Movement and High Church practices, which would probably have been opposed by Hall.

Gordon Lamp

Initially planned by local residents as an ornamental lamp for the Montpellier neighbourhood, following the death of General Gordon at Khartoum in 1885, another project was started to raise funds to erect a bronze statue in his honour at the junction of the Montpellier, Lansdown and Bayshill Roads. When the two projects were combined, however, only £20 was collected, largely because Gordon had no direct associations with the town. Further donations enabled residents to erect the lamp in 1887, where it still forms one of Cheltenham's most attractive pieces of street furniture. Originally lit by gas, it was converted to electricity by 1900 at the expense of a local resident.

Gordon Lamp.

W. G. Grace

Widely considered the 'father' of cricket and one of the world's greatest sporting personalities, Dr W. G. Grace (1848–1915) left an indelible mark on Cheltenham's cricket pitches. From an early age, between 1866 and 1870, as an accomplished Gloucestershire athlete, he also competed at tournaments in Cheltenham. However, his cricketing outshone his running ability. In August 1876, playing for Gloucestershire at Cheltenham College's ground, he achieved the highest individual innings in first class cricket when he scored 318 not out against Yorkshire, the second triple century he achieved within six days. As the Yorkshire cricketer Tom Emmett commented later, 'It was Grace before lunch, Grace after lunch, Grace all day.' It is said that, while aiming to hit sixes at both ends of the wicket at the College Ground, he kept his eye on the pavilion clock and then the main hospital entrance.

As a bowler, again when playing at Cheltenham, W. G. once took 7 Nottinghamshire wickets in just 17 balls. Known for his 'genial rascality', he was universally liked and always willing to share a joke. When one game finished early at Cheltenham, he memorably participated in a fun scratch game, Grace's XI playing with broomsticks against Frank Townsend's XI who played with bats. Even then, despite his handicap, W. G. succeeded in making a respectable score. Always looking for ways to improve his game, following his dictum to 'get at the bowler before the bowler gets you', on one occasion Grace visited Cheltenham to try out a new type of bat. In 1890, the spiral-handled bat, developed in the Cheltenham workshop of former Gloucestershire bowler William 'Woolfie' Woof, was, according to the *Cheltenham Chronicle*, set 'fair to create quite a sensation in the cricketing world'. Designed to afford the optimum balance with a not-too-heavy blade to improve cutting, driving and leg-hitting, the patented bat included a spiral spring packed with Indian rubber in the handle. When W. G. tried out the new bat, it was said that he 'expressed a very decided opinion as to its merits ... wishing some to be made and sent on to him'.

W. G.'s place in Cheltenham cricket history was further strengthened when he was asked to open the Victoria Cricket Ground, home of Cheltenham Cricket Club and occasional venue for Gloucestershire Cricket Club matches, on 21 June 1897. A year later he played his last Cheltenham Cricket Festival match at the age of fifty, scoring his last century for Gloucestershire at the College Ground. Twenty-six years earlier, he had played his first Cheltenham Festival match where he took 12 wickets for 63 runs and helped to beat Surrey by an innings. No wonder he is often regarded as the greatest cricketer that ever lived!

W. G. Grace at Cheltenham Cricket Festival, August 1898.

High Street

For a long time the only street in the town, the High Street was also known as the Great Street or Cheltenham Street in earlier times, often singled out by early visitors as an important feature. Johanna Schopenhauer, the mother of the German philosopher, for example, wrote in her *Travels in England and Scotland* (1803): 'Cheltenham consists of a single street, at least one mile long, from which small side streets radiate with single buildings. On this main street there are elegant buildings, glittering shops, lending libraries and cafés.' From the 1500s, it was the custom for water from the Chelt to be periodically diverted from the millpond at Cambray to flow down the centre of the High Street in order to cleanse it. Whenever this happened, pedestrians used stepping stones to cross the street. By 1786, however, the road was improved with a channel on either side for the water. During George III's visit in 1788, it became the departure point for the royal party, Fanny Burney recording in her diary: 'All Cheltenham was drawn out into the High-street, the gentles on one side and the commons on the other, and a band, and "God save the King," playing and singing'. As the town's popularity grew as a fashionable spa, following the king's visit,

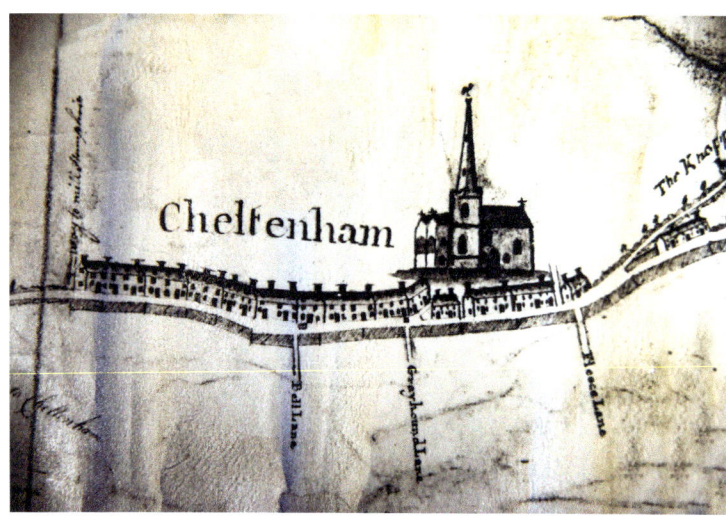

Cheltenham in 1776, showing its development along the High Street. (G. Coates)

the High Street provided a range of hotels and lodging houses, sometimes at excessive cost. Jane Austen, who visited the town for three weeks in 1816, was aggrieved to hear that her sister was charged 3 guineas a week for her lodging (at No. 85) and accused the landlady of charging for 'the *name* of the High Street'.

Gustav Holst

One of Cheltenham's most famous sons, the composer Gustav Holst (1874–1934) was born at No. 4 Pittville Terrace (now Clarence Road). He lived there for seven years until his mother's death in 1882, after which the family moved to No. 1 Vittoria Walk (the site now occupied by the telephone exchange). Originally built in 1832 as part of the Pittville Estate, Holst's birthplace is now a museum, celebrating his life and work through temporary and permanent displays that include both the piano on which much of *The Planets*, his most celebrated work, was composed, and original manuscripts dating from when Holst attended Cheltenham Grammar School. The house also depicts the upstairs-downstairs life typical of Victorian and Edwardian households, while the living room has been furnished in 1830s style, before the Holst family moved there, to convey the type of room in which Holst's grandfather, Gustavus Valentine von Holst (1799–1871), would have given harp and piano tuition to Cheltenham's young ladies. It appears that, as a baby, Gustav Holst had a dangerous encounter with a Pittville resident, who disliked prams. In 1875, Henry Swinhoe was fined £2 after assaulting Holst's nursemaid in Winchcombe Street by pushing his stick between the spokes of the wheels and attempting to knock over her pram.

Holst's musical talent was evident at an early age. When just four years old, he proclaimed to his father, who was organist at All Saints Church, 'That's my tune!' after his father played a tune on the organ, previously taught to him on the piano at home. Later, Gustav sang in the church choir, played violin or trombone in the church's orchestra and practised on the church organ, trying out new compositions, including *Four Voluntaries*, which he dedicated to his aunt Nina. Starting to compose from the age of twelve, Holst drew some inspiration from the streets of Cheltenham. His *Toccata* for piano, for example, was based on 'Newburn Lads', a Northumbrian pipe-tune he heard an old hurdy-gurdy man playing in 1879. As a teenager he composed the operetta *Lansdown Castle*, the original 'castle' being a crenellated building that once stood at the corner of Lansdown Road and Gloucester Road. At its première at the Corn Exchange (previously located on the High Street) on 11 February 1893, the *Gloucestershire Chronicle* portentously described it as 'remarkable and not unworthy of a trained and experienced musician'.

Although most of Holst's career from the age of seventeen took place outside Cheltenham, the town paid tribute to him by organising a festival of his works in 1927. Despite frail health Holst was able to conduct a performance of *The Planets* and, during the interval, was given a painting (now on display in the Holst Birthplace Museum) of Saturn, Neptune, Jupiter and Venus as seen from the top of Cleeve Hill

Music Room, Holst Birthplace Museum, including piano used to compose *The Planets*.

on 25 May 1919, the year then assumed to coincide with the first performance of *The Planets*. Holst described this as 'the most overwhelming event of my life'. In 2008, Cheltenham erected a fountain and statue in Holst's memory in Imperial Gardens. Interestingly, although right-handed, the statue shows Holst holding the baton in his left hand. This is because he suffered from neuritis in his right hand. It is also worth looking at the seven plaques incorporated into the octagonal plinth below which depict *The Planets*. These are arranged in an astrological, not astronomical order. Holst intended the orchestral suite to deal with the 'seven influences of destiny and constituents of our spirit' and arranged the planets in the following way, symbolising life's experiences and progression from youth to old age: Mars, the bringer of war; Venus, the bringer of peace; Mercury, the winged messenger; Jupiter, the bringer of jollity; Saturn, the bringer of old age; Uranus, the magician; and Neptune, the mystic.

George Holyoake

On 24 May 1842 the social reformer George Holyoake (1817–1906) gave a lecture at the Mechanics' Institute, then located in Albion Street opposite Pate's Almshouses. Following this, he became the last person in England to be imprisoned for blasphemy. Responding to a question about the place of religion in socialist communities, he commented that working families could ill afford a god and suggested that the deity be put on 'half pay' to save the poor from paying too much in church tithes. Accused of blasphemy after these remarks unintentionally made his audience laugh, Holyoake returned to the Mechanics' Institute on 2 June to defend his views at a meeting on free speech, but was arrested. At his trial he defended himself with a 9-hour speech, which he summarised as 'Christianity says we are all brethren, but I like not that equality which allows one man to revel in his opinions – while others are punished

Portrait of George Jacob Holyoake by Holyoake's nephew Rowland Holyoake, 1902.

with imprisonment in gaol for thinking theirs.' He was nevertheless convicted and sentenced to six months in Gloucester gaol. Later, he coined the word 'secularism', which he promoted as a morality separate from religious morality. Holyoake's association with Cheltenham resumed in 1864 when he returned, ironically, to try to deliver a lecture on *The Changes of Religious Opinion in England since 1841*. This time the venue was to be the Corn Exchange (behind No. 165 High Street). However, he was barred from lecturing here because of his earlier imprisonment. The lord of the manor arranged for the gas to be cut off at the Corn Exchange and also intimidated the owners of other local halls to prevent him from using them. Eventually, Holyoake delivered his lecture in a local inn.

Honeybourne Line

Today used as a cycle path, the Cheltenham part of the Honeybourne line was opened on 1 August 1906 as part of the Great Western Railway (GWR) line to connect Birmingham with the south-west. One main engineering achievement involved the construction of a 97-yard tunnel at Hunting Butts so that sufficiently wide ground could be retained for training horses there. Built after the town's considerable development, the line involved extensive disruption. Eight bridges were built, including one that cut through St George's Road, diverted part of Millbrook Street beneath it, and required the culverting of a stretch of the River Chelt and the demolition of a small cottage called Niagara on its banks. The remains of 400 graves from the Old Parish Cemetery, now redeveloped as Winston Churchill Memorial Gardens, had to be transferred to a different part of the ground, and a mortuary, which once existed in the cemetery, rebuilt into the fabric of the bridge traversing Market Street. All in all, around fifty houses in Great Western Road, Bloomsbury Place, White Hart Street (including the birthplace of the illusionist and inventor John Nevil Maskelyne), Carlton Place and Swindon Road (including the Cherry Tree Inn) were demolished and forty-two 'superior houses' built by the GWR in Alstone Lane. Further work was later carried out to level the site for a station and yard at Malvern Road station to avoid the need for locomotives to reverse from St James's station. This involved digging out 60,000 tons of earth and transferring it further north to form part of a half-mile-long embankment. Perhaps ominously, when the first train ran at 8:05 a.m. from St James's station, there were only six passengers. By March 1960 most local services between Cheltenham and Honeybourne had been withdrawn, with a residual service between Cheltenham, Stratford and Leamington surviving until 1968. Although it remained open for freight and diversionary traffic, the Cheltenham to Honeybourne line closed in 1976 after a section of the track was damaged by a derailed freight train. Since then a 22-mile-long section of the line, between Broadway and Cheltenham Racecourse has been reopened by the volunteer-operated Gloucestershire Warwickshire Railway.

Example of street art along the Honeybourne Line.

Entrance to the old mortuary rebuilt into the bridge traversing Market Street.

I

Ichthyosaurus Communis

While The Wilson houses the finest collection of fossils in Cheltenham, if not Gloucestershire, the Ladies' College also possesses an unusual specimen. Hanging on the wall in the college boarding house Fauconberg House in Bayshill Road is an ichthyosaur, believed to be approximately 185 million years old. The dark patch within its ribcage is thought to reflect the remains of the ichthyosaur's last meal. Ichthyosaurs were fish lizards that hunted in large numbers in the warm, shallow seas that covered the Cotswolds during the Jurassic period. They are a good example of a convergent species, half-fish and half-reptile, which could breathe air. While they show analogous structures to dolphins, sharks and tuna, they cannot be classed as fish. Thought to be the finest specimen of its type in the north Cotswolds, this ichthyosaur replaced one previously on display in the college museum, which loaned out specimens for teaching purposes between the

Ichthyosaur fossil, inside Fauconberg House.

1860s and 1930s. In 1899, this larger, though incomplete, ichthyosaur fossil was discovered near Malvern Road during construction of Glenlee, another of the college's boarding houses.

Imperial Gardens

Used as a commercial nursery at the beginning of the nineteenth century, the centre of Imperial Square was subsequently developed into a private pleasure garden for visitors to the Sherborne (later Imperial) Spa, which opened in 1818 on the site now occupied by the Queen's Hotel. Sometimes described as the 'jewel in Cheltenham's crown', the gardens still retain some earlier features, including balustraded stone steps. Missing, however, is a pagoda-shaped bandstand, erected there in 1920 adjacent to the Winter Garden. Built at a cost of £2,048, it was sold in 1948 to Bognor Regis for £175 where it can still be seen on the seafront. The gardens themselves, formally laid out just after the Second World War, now form an important site for the town's many festivals.

Balustraded stone steps, Imperial Gardens.

J

Edward Jenner

Although chiefly associated with his birthplace of Berkeley, further south in Gloucestershire, Edward Jenner (1749–1823) gained much influential support for his pioneering vaccination work through the close friends and associates he made in Cheltenham, then in its heyday as a spa town. Jenner first came to the town in 1795, living in the Lower High Street before moving a year later to No. 8 St George's Place (replaced by No. 22, rebuilt in facsimile on the original site), where he lived on a seasonal basis until 1820. Having previously developed his method of preventing smallpox through vaccination with cowpox, Jenner provided free vaccination clinics

Dr Jenner performing his first vaccination, 14 May 1796.

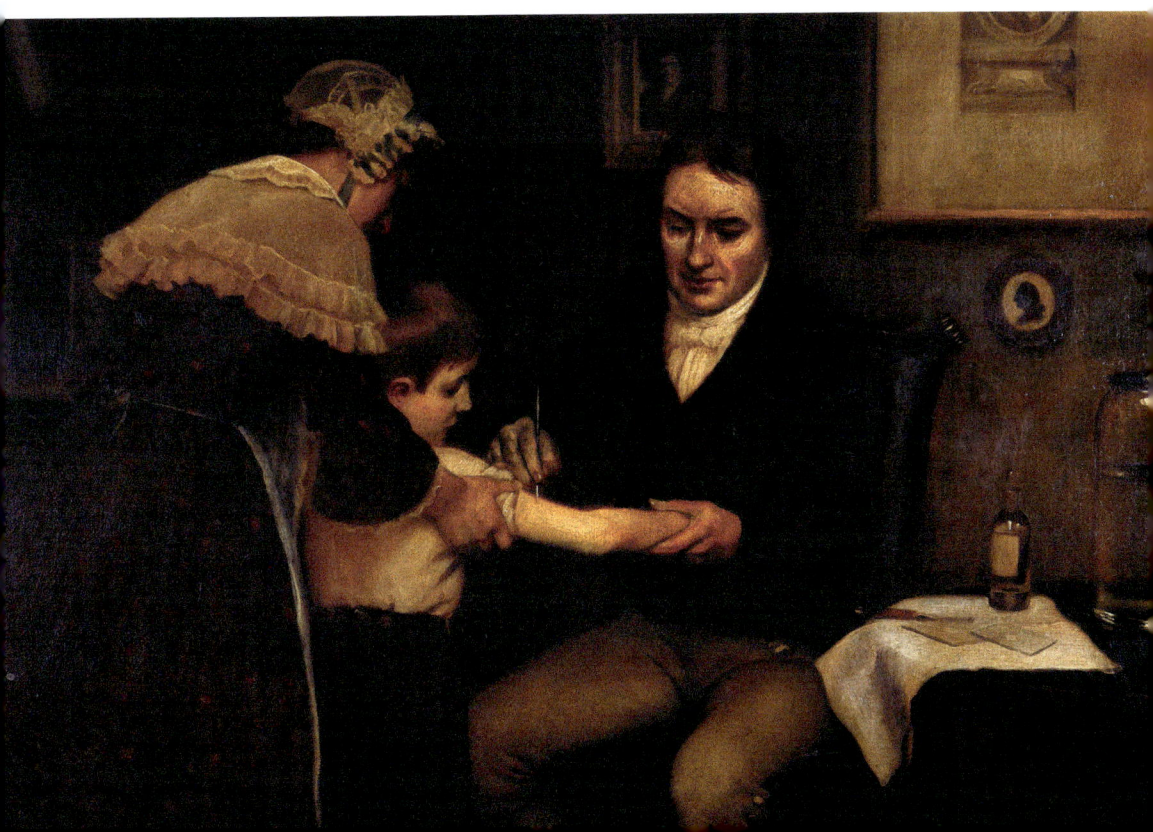

to the poor at Alpha House, nicknamed 'the Pest House', now Jenner Court (formerly Spirax Sarco) in St George's Road and, later, at Cheltenham Chapel after Sunday service. At times Jenner vaccinated up to 300 people a day in 1800, using lymph from cows kept on the slopes of Cleeve Hill. He later wrote, 'I permitted persons of all descriptions to come to me weekly. The smallpox was at their heels. I was literally mobbed, driven into a corner with: "The man shall do me next!", "No, he shan't – he shall do me."' In 1809 he claimed that he had successfully vaccinated 3,000–4,000 local people against smallpox during one epidemic. Opposite Jenner's former house is Jenner Walk, on the former site of his garden; beyond is the Cheltenham Chapel graveyard, restored as a Jenner memorial garden. Not impressed by the range of the town's 'medicinal' waters, Jenner was unconvinced of their health benefits. He wrote: 'It is really a very extraordinary Fact, that all the Medicinal Waters of any celebrity in the Island are to be found concentrated in this little Spot, Bath excepted, & to this I attach no more value than that which flows from my Tea Kettle.' Jenner also contributed to the town through establishing the town's Literary Society (later Literary and Philosophical Institution) and as one of the town commissioners. Jenner returned to Berkeley in 1815 following the death of his wife, preferring a quiet country life to the hubbub of fashionable life in Cheltenham. His ground-breaking discovery led not only to saving hundreds of millions of lives world-wide but also provided the basis for the modern science of immunology.

Jewish Burial Ground

In 1824 a small piece of land, later expanded to include adjoining land in Elm Street, was purchased in Worcester Row or Street to serve as the burial ground for the local synagogue. The earliest legible gravestone is dated 1833, although a Hebrew wall plaque also commemorates a four-month-old child who died eleven years earlier. The first recorded mention of Jews in Cheltenham was in 1749 when the *London Gazette* referred to a, probably itinerant, pedlar called Moses Myer. Although there was a thriving community in Gloucester, which reached its peak in the 1820s, it declined quickly from the 1830s as Cheltenham's community started to flourish. One possible factor in Gloucester's decline was the influx of Quakers, whose business acumen was viewed as a threat to the Jews. On the other hand, the Gloucester community was also attracted to Cheltenham after the upsurge in the town's fortunes following George III's visit in 1788.

Among the town's early Jewish traders was Jacob Abraham, who moved from Bath prior to 1814 to open a shop in Cheltenham. During one of several visits to Cheltenham, it was recorded that on 21 July 1828 the Duke of Wellington would 'sometimes [turn] into the shop of Mr Abraham, the optician, then adjoining the [Montpellier] Pump Room, where he would look at the barometer, and speculate with the old gentleman as to the sort of weather that was to be expected'. However, it was not just as an optician

The Jewish cemetery, Elm Street.

that Mr Abraham made his living. In September that year the *Cheltenham Journal* reported that the Duke 'repeatedly visited Mr Abraham's Emporium where he not only inspected the chief novelties and recent improvements, but condescendingly made some very large purchases'. This incident provided Abraham with valuable approval both from higher ranks and local townspeople. Other early settlers included Revd S. Lyon, a Hebrew teacher who lived at No. 2 St James's Street, and Dr Solomon Abraham Durlacher, who was born in Karlsruhe but worked in Cheltenham prior to 1808 as a 'Surgeon Dentist and Corn Operator', his son later becoming chiropodist to George IV, William IV, and Queen Victoria. In 1827 Isaiah Alex practised as a surgeon dentist at No. 414 (now No. 74) High Street, the *Cheltenham Journal* advertising his recently invented 'anodyne metallic cement' in 1830. He was a popular character whose patients included the Duke of Gloucester. He was well known for his philanthropy, the local press regularly advertising when he provided his services gratis to the poor. Another accomplished individual was Ivan Nestor-Schnurmann, thought to be the first teacher of Russian in a British school. He moved to Cheltenham College in 1892 where he opened and ran Corinth House (site now occupied by Century Court) as a small boarding house for Jewish boys. He retired in 1914.

Brian Jones

Cheltenham is recognised as part of rock music history through being the birthplace of Brian Jones (1942–69), the founding member of *The Rolling Stones*. Born in Rosemead at No. 17 Eldorado Road (commemorated by a Civic Society plaque), he attended Dean Close Junior School from 1947 to 1953 where he started piano lessons at the age of six. From 1953 to 1959, three years after his family moved to No. 335 Hatherley Road, he attended Cheltenham Grammar School (at its former High Street site), where he played clarinet in the school orchestra. Described then by a teacher as an 'intelligent rebel', his resentment of authority perhaps foreshadowed what was to come. A multitalented musician, he quickly learned to play the guitar, saxophone and harmonica, and joined local bands The Cheltenham 6 and The Ramrods. Although working briefly in Cheltenham as a trainee architect, music shop assistant and bus conductor, he set his heart on pursuing a musical career. After attending a concert of Alexis Korner's *Blues Incorporated* band at the Town Hall, he left Cheltenham for London in 1962 and, by July, had formed The Rollin' Stones (named after a Muddy Waters song), later The Rolling Stones.

Having by then mastered over thirty different types of musical instrument, Jones gave the band an extra dimension in their early years. His musical contribution included the band's unique guitar sound originally developed with Keith Richards. Known as the 'ancient art of weaving', it involved both guitarists playing rhythm and lead parts simultaneously without clear boundaries between the two roles. Jones returned to Cheltenham with The Rolling Stones several times from 1963 to 1965 to perform sell-out concerts at the Cheltenham Odeon. However, his success as a rock star and sex symbol came at a tragic cost. While under the influence of alcohol and drugs, he was found drowned in his swimming pool at the age of just twenty-seven. His funeral was held at St Mary's Church (now Cheltenham Minster). He was buried in the town's cemetery in Prestbury in a silver and bronze casket commissioned by his close friend Bob Dylan. Today, his grave is a place of pilgrimage for many of his fans. From 2005 a bust of him by Maurice Juggins has been on display in various venues in the town, most recently The Wilson.

Bust of 'Golden Boy' Brian Jones by Maurice Juggins.

K

The Knapp

Knapp Road and Knapp Lane, occupying a locality previously known as The Knapp, recall a Neolithic long barrow or knap (4000–2000 BC), which was excavated there in 1832. According to John Goding, Cheltenham's first historian, the naturally formed mound of earth had been hollowed out, within which a sepulchral chamber comprising three upright stones and a capstone, later used as a cider press, was discovered. The tomb was said to contain various fragments, including broken urns, burnt human bones, stone implements and personal ornaments. The site was cleared in 1846 when the St James's railway station was completed. Another knap on Shurdington

The knap that survives on Shurdington Hill.

Hill, off Greenway Lane, excavated before 1779, is still visible today, while another knap feature once existed in Knavenhill field (today near Avenall Parade, off Old Bath Road), Charlton Kings.

William Hill Knight

One of the town's most accomplished architects, William Hill Knight (1814–95), moved to Cheltenham by at least 1835 after marrying Matilda Hastings there. Initially, he went into partnership with another architect Rowland Paul, during which he produced designs for the classical-style Cheltenham synagogue. Later, after setting up his own business, he designed Cheltenham Grammar School, commemorated at No. 111 Lower High Street by a Civic Society plaque. His other work includes the Cheltenham College Baths and lodge in Sandford Road, two college boarding houses, and the main building in Dean Close School. He may also have contributed to the completion of Montpellier Walk (1843–60), designed by Robert and Charles Jearrad, which helped to establish Cheltenham as a fashionable shopping centre. His most highly acclaimed work is the Public Library building in Clarence Street. He is buried in the local cemetery.

Portrait of William Hill Knight, possibly by Ada Grudelach.

L

Lamp Standards

Several unusual lamp standards can still be seen throughout the town. Those with the most dramatic and idiosyncratic style, known affectionately as 'dragon and onion', were designed by the borough engineer, Joseph Hall (1851–1914), in the 1890s. Responsible for designing many of the town's much-loved buildings, including the Neptune Fountain, the boathouse by Pittville lake, the refreshment kiosk in Pittville's

Below left: 'Dragon and Onion' lamp standard.

Below right: 'Tall Twins' lamp standard, with detail of base (inset).

long garden and the 'Strozzi Palace' (originally the main electricity distribution centre in St George's Place, now converted into apartments), Hall displays a sense of aesthetics, practicality and jest in the legacy of his street lamps. Comprising an onion-shaped finial with an arched lamp holder with dragon infill, examples of this unique style can still be seen in the minster's churchyard and Trafalgar Street. Another early high-quality design, aptly named 'Tall Twins', was used to suspend lamps between pairs of very high standards, which rose above the thoroughfares' trees. These standards required large bases, attractively decorated with the town's coat of arms, pigeons and acanthus leaves, to accommodate the equipment required to transform the electrical current to the right voltage. Originally used in the Promenade, one example can today be seen near the Lido. While a range of other designs were later used, none since match the exquisite character of those resembling 'dragon and onion' and 'Tall Twins'.

Lido

One of the town's most popular attractions, the Lido in Sandford Park serves as one of the oldest and largest outdoor heated swimming pools in the country. Built in 1935 after the site was dug out by Irish labourers, it attracted 100,000 visitors during its first season. Its name, deriving from *litus* (Latin meaning 'shore') and evoking the famous Venetian seaside resort, helped to promote the idea of a shared space where men, women and children in all sectors of society could come together for informal relaxation. Today the concept of public health and inclusion for all is still central to the Lido's philosophy. During the Second World War the facility provided an important place for recuperation for wounded soldiers, its car park used as a petrol depot for passing military convoys. During the 1970s the advent of cheap foreign package holidays coupled with severe budgetary constraints threatened its closure. To make matters worse, in Cheltenham's case, subsequent architectural

The Irish labourers who dug out the site in 1935.

surveys during the 1980s and 1990s revealed signs of serious structural damage. However, a major refurbishment programme carried out in 2006–07 has helped to restore the Lido to its former glory. Ten years later, annual attendance levels soared to more than 210,000.

Lido fountain, originally serving to aerate and purify the water.

William Charles Macready

The celebrated Shakespearean actor William Charles Macready (1793–1873) lived in the Tudor-Gothic-style terrace at No. 6 Wellington Square from 1860 until his death. A statue believed to be of Macready is located on the upper façade of the house. Macready was not only the leading actor of his day but also a close friend of Charles Dickens, who stayed at his house when he visited Cheltenham to give public readings of his work. Macready, although retired, also gave readings and lectures in Cheltenham which he considered had 'conveniences of all kinds equal those of London'. Commenting on the town's beauty, he wrote: 'I do not think there is a town in England, or out of it, laid out with so much taste, such a continual intermixture of garden, villa, street and avenue.' He made earlier visits to Cheltenham during a holiday in 1801 and, as an actor, in 1821 and 1836 when he played Hamlet and Virginius at the Theatre Royal (a site now occupied by the Ladies' College Princess Hall). His brother, Major Edward Nevil Macready, who commanded all that was left of the Light Company of the 30th Regiment towards the end of the Battle of Waterloo, is buried in Leckhampton churchyard.

Statue, believed to be of Macready, at No. 6 Wellington Square.

St Margaret's Terrace, a part of Katherine Monson's continuing legacy.

Monson Avenue

Of all the builders involved in developing Cheltenham in its early years, by far the most unusual was Katherine Monson (1754–1843), the daughter of the 2nd Baron Monson of Burton in Lincolnshire. It is thought that she moved to Cheltenham by the 1790s, buying land north of the High Street at the beginning of the nineteenth century. Her interest in building was already evident at the end of the eighteenth century when she rented her own house, Monson Villa, in St Margaret's Road. Today, although the villa was demolished in 1871, part of Monson Avenue car park recalls the site. Monson's subsequent building projects included a house called St Margaret's which, before it was destroyed in 1940 during a Second World War bombing raid, served as the ticket office for the Black & White coach company. Unusually for a member of the titled gentry, particularly a woman, Monson was fully engaged in the building process, providing active support and supervision for her projects, even into her sixties. In all, it is thought that she built at least seventeen houses in the town, including St Margaret's Terrace and houses in Albert Place and Prestbury Road. Unfortunately, like so many builders during the late 1820s, she became heavily in debt and then bankrupt following the 1825 banking crisis. Fleeing to France to avoid her creditors, she later returned to Cheltenham, where she stayed with her former clerk of works, William Halford, in North Place, not far from the buildings she constructed in St Margaret's Terrace. She died at the age of eighty-nine and was subsequently buried in Halford's family grave, visible outside the west door of Holy Trinity Church.

Montpellier Gardens

Originally laid out in 1831, Montpellier Gardens were conceived as exclusive pleasure grounds for visitors to Montpellier Spa but were acquired by Cheltenham Borough Council in 1893. The gardens have hosted several important events in

A–Z of Cheltenham

the town's history, including notable balloon ascents. One of these occurred on 22 September 1837 when Margaret Graham (née Watson), already the first British woman to make a solo balloon flight, in 1828, accompanied Mr Garrett, the landlord of the White Lion, on one of the first mixed gender aerial ascents on record. Equally enthralling for the watching crowd was the sight of a small wicker basket containing Mrs Graham's chimpanzee 'Mademoiselle Jennie' attached beneath the balloon and equipped with a parachute. As the balloon entered clear space beyond the Lansdown estate, Mrs Graham cut the connecting cord from the wicker basket, causing 'Mademoiselle Jennie' to plummet towards the ground. The week before, the designer of the same parachute had met an unfortunate end when the ripcord failed; this time the parachute worked successfully and the chimpanzee landed safely in a field near the Lansdown Turnpike Gate. Graham and Garrett descended in a field in Hartpury and returned to Cheltenham to be reunited with 'Mademoiselle Jennie' and celebrate the event in the Beehive pub, Montpellier Villas. Other notable events include the first successful parachute descent made by an Englishman (John Hampton) on 3 October 1838 and the founding of the local archery club in 1857 by Horace Ford, regarded as the 'father of modern archery'.

Montpellier Rotunda

In 1817 Henry Thompson, the developer of Montpellier Spa, commissioned George Allen Underwood, the architect of the Masonic Hall and Holy Trinity Church, to design a new stone building to replace the original Montpellier pump room of 1809. This included the crouching lion that still adorns the parapet. Given his entrepreneurial spirit, Thompson would probably not have been surprised that his exquisite building was later used for other purposes, including a bank

Cheltenham Archery Club, Montpellier Gardens, 22 September 1910.

and, today, a restaurant. It was Thompson who sank hundreds of wells, which provided a variety of different types of water, each with their individual mineral compositions, characteristics, and strengths. The fact that there were six springs that fed Thompson's spa was noted in 1819 by one of the spa's earliest visitors, the thirteen-year-old poet Elizabeth Barrett (later Browning). Barrett's visit predated the crowning glory of the building, the addition of its copper-sheathed dome which, commissioned by Thompson's son Pearson and completed in 1826, gave the building its name – the Rotunda. Modelled on similar proportions to Rome's Pantheon, the dome was designed by the architect John Papworth who also designed some of the houses in Montpellier Parade, Lansdown and part of St James's Church in Suffolk Square. Soon afterwards the Rotunda became an important centre for Cheltenham's social and cultural life. There was the visit by Arthur Wellesley, 1st Duke of Wellington in 1828 when he attended a Promenade Ball. There were also prestigious concerts, including by Theodor Döhler, a famous German composer in his day, Jenny Lind, the Swedish opera singer, and Franz Liszt, who disappointingly, according to one local critic, only played to an audience of around 220, and whose performance was marred by the poor acoustics in the Rotunda. The Rotunda also served as an important venue for Cheltenham's own highly accomplished musical family, the Holsts (or von Holsts as they were known prior to the First World War). Gustav's father Adolph often directed chamber concerts and gave piano recitals here, particularly during the 1870s and 1880s, while Gustav premièred several of his own compositions, including his *Duet in D* for two pianos which he performed with his father in 1899. Housing such activities as flower shows, magic shows, private theatricals, and meetings of local societies, the Rotunda later became used for an increasing number of commercial activities. The Worcester City and County Bank set up its operation in one corner of the building from 1882. Lloyds bank took over in the 1920s, and bought the building in 1962.

The Pump Room at Thompson's Montpellier Spa.

N

Sir Charles Napier

One of the distinguished soldiers who, for a time, resided in Cheltenham was General Sir Charles James Napier (1782–1853). Soon after his arrival on 21 September 1848, he became a prominent figure in the town's social circles. From his house near Imperial Square at No. 1 Wolseley Terrace he rode about the town on the Arab horse upon which he had fought many battles in India, and mixed with numerous officers, including Lord Ellenborough, who had served with him there. Following the Duke of Wellington's famous request ('If you don't go, I must') that Napier should return to India to deal with renewed unrest in the Punjab, a farewell dinner was held in

Sir Charles Napier, by Charles Mercier, displayed at the Queen's Hotel.

his honour at the Queen's Hotel on 5 October. Nevertheless, Napier did not leave Cheltenham until 13 March 1849, receiving rapturous applause from the crowd watching his departure at the railway station.

The Neptune Fountain

This ornate sculpture, designed by borough engineer Joseph Hall, was influenced by the Trevi Fountain in Rome. Carved in 1893 by R. L. Boulton, it shows Neptune, the Roman god of the sea, with horses and tritons. When the council planned to site the fountain outside the Imperial Rooms (now Royscott House), a dispute arose with W. A. Powell, the owner of the rooms who used them then as a warehouse. Powell claimed that the fountain would detract from the value of the Imperial Rooms but lost his legal case and the fountain was built. Today, the water of the fountain is still fed from the River Chelt, which flows directly underneath. The model who sat for the figure of Neptune was Dick Saunders, a local labourer of fine physique employed by the corporation. Described in the *Cheltenham Chronicle* in 1919 at the time of

The Neptune Fountain.

his death as a 'tough nut to crack', Saunders was well-known as a leader in the local labourers' trade union and a Conservative stalwart who supported Sir James Agg-Gardner, Cheltenham's MP during four separate periods between 1874 and 1928. His obituary commented perhaps diplomatically that 'his political principles could be enforced by biceps when necessary, and he had, in fact, a weakness for this method of persuasion'. Earlier newspaper reports recall court cases when Saunders was charged with being drunk and disorderly and assaulting a policeman, and another when a dealer in old iron threatened to find someone to fight Saunders, even 'if he had to send 50 miles for the man to do it, or pay £30 for the job!'

Normal Terrace

This unusually named street, between the High Street and Swindon Road, was originally known as Beckingsale's Passage after a well-known grocer's shop on the High Street that produced the 'celebrated Royal Cheltenham sausages'. By c. 1874, however, it had changed to its present name, reflecting the fact that the Church of England Normal College (now part of University of Gloucestershire's Francis Close campus), located opposite, had been built. Constructed in 1849, largely by the efforts of Revd Francis Close, the Normal College provided education for teachers, 'normal' referring to the fact that its students learned to teach within an established set of educational standards – known as 'norms'. Later, it became known as St Paul's Teacher Training College, its female department being located in the former General Hospital site (now Normandy House) on the Lower High Street. Amusingly, one of the houses in the terrace is called Odd Cottage.

Cheltenham Normal College (from *Norman's History of Cheltenham*, 1863).

Norwood Triangle

Located at the intersection between Norwood Road, Grafton Road, Andover Road and Great Norwood Street, is the 'Norwood Triangle'. This was a focal point for a tramroad for horse-drawn wagons, which brought stone and other materials from Leckhampton Hill and Gloucester Docks for the building of South Town, the artisan district that developed around Bath Road, Tivoli and The Suffolks. Today a series of circular engraved stones set in the triangular paved area tell the story of the Leckhampton to Cheltenham branch of the tramroad, which traversed what is now Leckhampton Road, Norwood Road, Andover Road and Queen's Road.

Great Norwood Street was the line of a siding that previously connected the Norwood triangle with stonemasons' yards. It was the first railway in the county authorised by an Act of Parliament. Operating from 1810 until 1861, when it closed following competition from railway expansion and the nuisance caused to road vehicles, at its peak the tramroad made up to sixty journeys each day carrying over 35,000 tons of general materials and 20,000 tons of stone from the Leckhampton quarries in a single year. Different toll rates were charged for different types of goods, from 8½d per ton for manure and stone for road repairs, to more than 2s a ton for coal, stone and beer, and 3s for manufactured goods. A plaque at the site commemorates the Railway Inn, which served the working community from 1836 to 1968.

Four engraved stones at the Norwood Triangle.

Old Bath Road

One of the town's most ancient routes, there is even speculation that, as an extension of Hales Road, it once connected the Iron Age settlements of Crickley Hill and Leckhampton Hill with the Cleeve Hill camp. Although records from 1290 refer to it as Edge Way, by 1350, along with Hales Road, it was called the *via regis* (King's Highway). On 3 May 1471 this was the route taken by Edward IV and his 3,000 infantrymen as they arrived to stay in the town overnight before fighting the Battle of Tewkesbury the following day. Despite the route's importance it had fallen into disrepair by 1629, the Cheltenham Manor Court Books recording that '*alta via ducens versus Sandfords bridge ... in magna ruina*'. Perhaps this was not surprising since recorded

Old Bath Road looking south from the Wheatsheaf.

O

infringements on the *via regis* included digging and ploughing, obstruction with timbers and dungheaps, tree growth and the construction of houses. Its present name probably derived from around George III's visit in 1788. Although a 1617 guidebook referred to it as the 'road from Cirencester and Bath', in the pre-turnpike era it would not have been considered a natural route to Bath in particular. Its name was certainly established by 1813 when the construction of the parallel New Bath Road (now Bath Road) began running from Cambray to Leckhampton and thence to Bath.

Old Well Walk

Formerly one of the notable, much illustrated features of the town, the Old Well Walk, also once referred to as the Long Walk, is today represented only by the short pedestrian Well Walk (off Clarence Street). This gravelled promenade, originally 20 feet wide, lined with elms and limes, was inspired by a similar avenue at Hotwells in Bristol. Laid out in 1738–42 by Captain Henry Skillicorne, the developer of the spa, it served to link the parish churchyard, and High Street, with the Old (or Original) Well, that now lies beneath Cheltenham Ladies' College. Roughly aligning slightly west of the present-day Montpellier Street and then following the axis along Royal Crescent and Crescent Place, its drastic curtailment is a good example of how the spa's fortunes suddenly declined from the 1830s.

The Old Well Walk, by Henry Lamb, *c.* 1825.

A–Z of Cheltenham

Outdoor Meeting Places

Part of Cheltenham's history, particularly from 1850 to 1950, is evident through some of the outdoor meetings held at various locations throughout the town. These typically supported political and other campaigns and issues for public debate. Traditional street meeting places included the corners of Exmouth Street (at Bath Road) and Copt Elm Road (at London Road). Other focal points were open spaces near public houses such as the Norwood Arms, or churches such as St Paul's. One of the largest gatherings occurred on 22 September 1922 in the playground of the Grammar School (then located in the High Street) when David Lloyd George addressed a crowd estimated at approximately 11,000 for 80 minutes on behalf of the local (unsuccessful) Liberal candidate Sir John Brunner. Meetings were also held at strategically sited lamps, including the Hewlett Lamp (corner of Leighton Road).

However, the most significant central meeting place was the Clarence Street lamp, installed *c.* 1900 at the junction with Imperial Circus. This became the traditional place for revellers to celebrate the new year. Following the ringing of the parish church bells, people danced around the lamp – sometimes in snow, sometimes in mud – and sang 'Auld Lang Syne'. It was also a place of protest. Four days after the execution of the radical Spanish thinker Francisco Ferrer on 13 October 1909

The Clarence Street Lamp.

several hundred protesters gathered at the lamp to 'place on record [the people of Cheltenham's] detestation of the infamous crime of the Spanish Government in murdering ... Spain's most honoured citizen'. As an exposed venue for meetings the Clarence Lamp occasionally witnessed physical clashes. In the run-up to the Cheltenham by-election in 1911 the Liberals and the suffragettes both sought to speak here. After arriving first, the suffragettes were already addressing the crowd from a cart when the Liberals appeared. The suffragettes refused to move and continued talking while the crowd threatened to bodily remove the cart. Eventually, the police led the cart away, with the suffragettes still speaking! Two years later, an angry mob disrupted a suffragists' meeting there with hand bells. Under the headline 'Cheltenham Disgraced' the *Cheltenham Chronicle* reported, 'Respected citizens ..., engaging in a constitutional manner, were assailed with vegetables in varying stages of putrefaction, and eggs and epithets equally vile, and had their meeting broken up in disorder without a single speech having been delivered'. During the First World War several soldier recruitment drives were held there, sometimes accompanied by bands playing patriotic music and, at other times, with war pictures shown on a 20-by-18-foot screen. On 25 June 1915 an estimated crowd of 2,000 was present for the mass recruitment meeting for the 11th Gloucesters. On another occasion the 'Laureate of Gloucestershire' poet Will Harvey was among the soldiers who addressed the crowd.

From the 1920s onwards the increasing noise from passing buses led some groups to change their regular meeting venue from the Clarence Lamp to the Neptune Fountain. It was here that the Cheltenham Communist Party held open-air meetings during the 1930s and 1940s. On another occasion, one of their high-profile (but less than enthusiastic) members, the poet Cecil Day-Lewis, was relieved to discover that the scheduled meeting by the fountain had been cancelled, sparing him the task of introducing the invited speaker.

The suffragist Rosa Swiney speaking at the Clarence Street Lamp in 1911.

P

Parabola Road

Curved in an approximate U-shape with some degree of mirror-symmetry, this appropriately named road is thought to be unique in England. Its unusual form creates a sense of intrigue, as the road constantly changes, rising and curving simultaneously. Also of note are the unusually large junctions it creates with Bayshill Road and Overton Road because of its shape. First developed from *c.* 1839, when the Queen's Parade section was started, the road was then simply known as The Parabola. However, as with the rest of the Bayshill Estate, financial difficulties dogged its initial development. Following the bankruptcy of its builder, William Swain, the construction of the Queen's Parade terrace ceased in 1846, and was not fully finished until the mid-1980s, nearly 140 years later!

Parabola Road from the Bayshill Road end.

Richard Pate

Richard Pate (1516–88) is best remembered as one of the town's most important philanthropists, largely through founding the grammar school (now in Princess Elizabeth Way) and an almshouse (now in Albion Street). Described by the antiquarian Thomas Dudley Fosbroke as 'a very excellent and charitable man', he is thought to have attended the chantry school attached to the parish church before studying at Corpus Christi College, Oxford. In 1541, he joined Lincoln's Inn. Initially becoming a barrister, he later served as Recorder of Gloucester and the city's MP. Recognising through his work with the Charity Commissioners the need to support education for the middle classes, his plans to establish a *Schola Grammatica* found favour with Queen Elizabeth I who gave him a grant of land and property in 1574 'for the perpetual maintenance and foundation of a free Grammar School … and also a Hospital or Almshouse for six old poor people, of whom two were to be women'. In 1586, he transferred some of his own property, together with that previously granted by Elizabeth, to his old college for the endowment of the school and almshouse.

Statue of Richard Pate at Pate's Grammar School, Princess Elizabeth Way.

Penfold Pillar Boxes

Among the town's more unusual features are its cast-iron Penfold pillar boxes, some of the earliest in the country. Designed by architect J. W. Penfold in 1865, the attractive hexagonal boxes with a decorative beaded cap surmounted by a 6-inch acanthus bud were installed from September 1866. Originally painted green, they were restyled in red in 1874 to make them more visible. Today, Cheltenham has a group of seven original boxes located at the following sites: Bayshill Road (at junction with Parabola Road), Douro Road (at corner with Malvern Place), Evesham Road (corner of Cleevelands Drive), Hewlett Road (corner of Pittville Circus Road), Lansdown Road (corner of Westall Green and Queen's Road), Montpellier Walk, and St Paul's Road (corner of Margaret Road). The Cheltenham group of boxes is rare since only around twenty of the original 1866 boxes are left throughout the country. Now Grade II listed, they were made by the Dudley-based firm of Cochrane Grove & Co. An additional one is housed in The Wilson's collections.

The pillar box in Bayshill Road.

Sir Thomas Phillipps

One of the town's most eccentric characters was the obsessive collector of books and manuscripts Sir Thomas Phillipps (1792–1872). Buying at a rate of forty to fifty items per week, Phillipps acquired approximately 50,000 books and 60,000 manuscripts in his lifetime. At one stage, he even aimed to acquire a copy of every book in the world and coined the term 'vello-maniac' to describe his life's obsession. In 1863 he rented Thirlestaine House, the Bath Road mansion previously used by Lord Northwick as a home and art gallery, to house his vast collection. Phillipps' move was motivated by a family rift, particularly his concern that his son-in-law should not acquire his rare manuscripts. Nevertheless, the logistics of moving arguably the largest collection a single individual had ever created were complex. Between July 1863 and March 1864, it took over 100 wagonloads using 230 horses accompanied by 160 men to transport it across the Cotswolds from Broadway to Cheltenham.

Phillipps' obsession came at a cost to his family. In Thirlestaine House, which he bought in 1867, his second, and long-suffering, wife Elizabeth Mansel complained that she was 'booked out of one wing and ratted out of the other'. With her husband's refusal to spend money on anything but his collection, Thirlestaine House became an uncomfortable place in which to live. Elizabeth's health failed, and she spent some time recuperating in a boarding house in Torquay where she lamented how happy she would be if he stopped setting his heart so much on his books! His youngest daughter, Kate, and her family refused to stay at Thirlestaine House because they found it too cold and uncomfortable. Henrietta, his eldest daughter, commented that her father originally planned to build a circular room, similar to the British Museum Reading Room, at Thirlestaine House so that he could find his books easily. However, this never materialised and much of his collection remained unpacked in packing cases,

Thirlestaine House, where Thomas Phillips lived from 1863 to 1872.

with the result that he found it difficult to find anything, having to rely on handwritten notes to support his ailing memory.

Although Phillipps' obsession contributed to unhappy family relationships, it undoubtedly helped to save some rare manuscripts, including the original orders, now held in the National Maritime Museum at Greenwich, signed by Philip II to send the Spanish Armada against England. Following Phillipps's death in 1872, Thirlestaine House and its contents were left in trust to Kate and her third son, Thomas Fitzroy Fenwick, but without any income to maintain it. The will stipulated that the collection was to remain intact and not to be moved from there. However, thirteen years later judicial approval was given to break the trust. After reorganising and recataloguing the collection, Kate's son gradually sold it off over the next fifty years, although final dispersal was to take around 100 years in total. Today, examples from the collection are present in many of the world's major libraries and museums. The sale raised assets of around £1.6 million. Sir Thomas Phillipps also succeeded in putting Cheltenham on the world map as scholars continue to reference many of his collection's most valuable manuscripts either by 'Cheltenham Codex' or 'Codex Cheltenhamensis'.

Pittville

Begun in 1824, Pittville Estate was named by its developer Joseph Pitt (1759–1842). Reputedly helped as a boy to pursue a legal career by an attorney impressed by the sharpness of his mind, Pitt's first job involved charging gentlemen a penny to hold their horses. At first his Pittville venture appeared a well-calculated risk. Between 1801 and 1821 the town's population had increased fourfold to 13,388 which, coupled with an increase in visitors, created a huge demand for housing. His vision was meticulously planned, allowing, for example, only certain professions (librarians, nurserymen, coffee housekeepers and florists) to operate within the 100-acre estate, and six shops to be restricted to Prestbury Road. However, by 1860 Pitt's vision of a new town on the northern edge had floundered. Less than a third of the houses planned had been constructed, partly due to the post-1825 economic slump, the decline in the fashion for taking the waters, and the estate's relative distance from the town centre. Despite this, significant success had been achieved. Following her visit in 1833, Scottish author Catherine Sinclair described Pittville as 'a scene of gorgeous magnificence […] sprinkled with houses of every size, shape and character: Grecian temples, Italian villas, and citizen's boxes, so fresh and clean, you would imagine they were all blown out at once like soap bubbles'. Although Pitt died in great debt, his architectural legacy remains one of the highest quality in Cheltenham, and Pittville one of the finest examples of a 'Regency' estate.

Central to the estate's appeal was the Pump Room, reckoned by some to be England's finest spa building, and its adjoining gardens, which were laid out in 1827. Built by John Forbes in 1825–30, the Pump Room incorporated impressive Ionic columns, based on the Athenian Temple on the Ilissus, and parapet figures (now copies of the originals) of

View from Pittville Park bandstand.

Hippocrates, 'father' of medicine, Hygeia, goddess of health, and Aesculapius, god of medicine and healing. Originally, its lessee paid Pitt an annual fee, which allowed him to charge subscribers for the sale of spa water, entry to the gardens and attendance at special events. Among the attractions in 1837–40 were a tightrope walker, who crossed Pittville Lake 40 feet above its surface; Isaac A. Van Amburgh, an American animal trainer, who exhibited an elephant swimming across the lake; and Madame Rosini who ascended and descended a 50-foot-high rope among fireworks and coloured lights! Upon Pitt's death in 1842, the Pump Room became part of his debt-ridden estate, and was eventually bought from the bank by the borough council in 1889. Thereafter, its future remained uncertain. At one time, its ballroom even functioned as a badminton hall. During the Second World War, it served as a storage depot for the US Army, the neglect and damage caused during this period almost leading to its demolition. Restoration work began in 1949 and it was reopened in 1960 by the 7th Duke of Wellington, whose earlier ancestor, the 1st Duke, had witnessed its construction. Today, the Pump Room is one of the town's major venues for public and private events. The pump which draws water from the 80-foot-well was thoroughly overhauled in the 1970s, and staff endeavour to ensure the waters are always available. Its park now contains more than 850 trees, including a 14-metre-high Pencil Cedar (*Juniperus virginiana*), the largest in the UK.

Post Offices

Writing in 1876, the *Cheltenham Chronicle* mused that the town's 'Post Office casts off its old quarters periodically as a crab casts his shell'. Prior to the first private post office being established by a grocer in 1800 on the north side of the High Street near

The post office at Nos 33–41 Promenade.

Pittville Street, the postal service was, according to Cheltenham's first historian John Goding, at the mercy of an eccentric woman who, in the evenings after finishing work, delivered mail 'at least within a fortnight after they left the place from whence they were sent'. During the early years, the site of the post office changed frequently along the High Street. Despite normally occupying a central position, it ranged at times from the corner with Park Street in the Lower High Street to the entrance to Grosvenor Street at the upper end. It also moved to Regent Street and, in 1842, to Clarence Street. By the early 1860s demand for an efficient service had increased considerably, with around two million letters being delivered annually to Cheltenham residents, an operation employing twenty-three permanent staff.

On 18 December 1876 the post office moved to Nos 33–41 Promenade (now Waterstones), previously occupied by the Imperial Club, formerly the Imperial Hotel. A large public hall was created by converting the two lower storeys into one. Telegraphic messages were sent from an upstairs room, instructions being sent from the ground floor via pneumatic tubes, which doubled up as speaking tubes. The service road at the back of the building, named Post Office Lane from at least 1883, was used by carts to deliver and collect the mail. Further reconstruction and enlargement took place in 1904–06, during which the post office was temporarily relocated to the King's Hall (now demolished) in North Street, and in 1932 when, it is thought, synthetic marble tiles were used for the first time as flooring for a post office building in the country. By then a teleprinter service had been installed, and telegrams were typed rather than handwritten. Since its closure there in 1987, the post office has occupied two further different High Street locations.

The Promenade

Cheltenham's most fashionable thoroughfare (originally called Sherborne Walk) was once nothing more than a scarcely passable marshy track. In 1818 landowners Samuel Harward and Thomas Henney laid out a tree-lined avenue connecting the High Street with the Sherborne (later Imperial) Spa on the site now occupied by the Queen's Hotel.

The Upper Promenade (George Rowe, 1840).

In its early days the Promenade was for subscribers only. By the end of the 1820s, considerable development had taken place, including the establishment in 1826 of the Promenade's first shop, Clark and Debenham (now called Cavendish House), which still occupies its original, though now enlarged, site. Once described by the *Times* as 'perhaps the most beautiful thoroughfare in the country', the Promenade creates an interesting optical illusion through its width, its upper end being twice the size of its lower end. As a result, the town centre appears farther from the Queen's Hotel, but viewed from the High Street end the distance seems shorter.

Prestbury Park

Representing the 'Park Lane' property in the Gloucestershire edition of the Monopoly board game, Prestbury Park goes back to at least 1136 when it was a hunting park owned by John, Bishop of Hereford, its name being recorded as 'parc de Presteburye' in 1464. The first steeplechase was held in Prestbury Park in 1834 when it was owned by Lord Ellenborough. It was not until 1898 that it became the permanent home for Cheltenham's races.

General view of Prestbury Park.

Q

Quaker Burial Ground

Located in Grove Street (for a time known as Day Lane), off the Lower High Street, the Quaker Burial Ground is one of Cheltenham's oldest surviving features. Although its blocked-off entrance bears the date 1700, the ground was acquired in 1682. A small Quaker community existed in the town from 1658. By the time George Fox, the founder of the Religious Society of Friends (or Quakers) visited the town twenty years later, it was said he addressed 'a large gathering'. Before the Toleration Act of 1689, several Cheltenham Quakers were fined or imprisoned for attending illegal meetings. They included Elizabeth Sandford, who was jailed and punished 'in the flesh, oft times severely' for allowing her property to be used for Quaker services. In 1682, in search of religious freedom, fifteen of the town's Quakers, including Richard Wall and Tobias Leach, emigrated to America where, on land belonging to William Penn of Pennsylvania fame, they established the township of Cheltenham. By 1702, however, a Quaker Meeting House was established in Manchester Walk (now part of Clarence Street) near the site of the old Shaftesbury Hall (now Chelsea Square), replaced in 1836 on neighbouring land. A new meeting house was built at North House, Portland Street in 1903 and, since 1985, the current premises are located in Warwick Place. Today the burial ground is used as a fencing manufacturer, the last burials having

The Quakers' burial ground entrance in Grove Street.

been made prior to 1870. Part of the original Cotswold stone wall survives, much weathered. Among those buried there is Elizabeth Skillicorne (d. 1779), the daughter of Quaker William Mason, who owned the field where Cheltenham's spa waters were first discovered. Elizabeth, who is recalled on her husband's commemorative tablet in Cheltenham Minster as 'A Virtuous Woman, A good Wife & tender Mother', married Captain Henry Skillicorne, who developed Cheltenham's first spa.

Quarries

Quarrying has taken place in Cheltenham's surrounding hills since ancient times. On Cleeve Hill, quarry waste was found to contain two Roman coins dated AD 293, while detailed quarrying records date from 1389. Some of the oldest quarry workings even fooled certain eminent Victorian geologists into believing that the town's south-western-facing cliffs represented the coastline of an ancient sea, which they called 'the Malvern Straits'. On Leckhampton Hill it is estimated that between the 1790s and 1920s over 2 million tons of different rock types were extracted (aided early on by the first-known goods railway in the county, a horse-drawn tramway, which opened in 1810). Accidents frequently occurred, sometimes caused by local residents riding in empty trucks to avoid a steep climb up the hill, then facing danger when the windlass rope broke! In the 1820s–30s the main stone depot (known as Grotten's Wharf) was located on the corner of Great Norwood Street and Suffolk Road (then called Commercial Road). Among the stone extracted at Leckhampton was Inferior Oolite freestone, known as 'Cheltenham Stone', which was used for Cheltenham's classical Regency architecture. Today, some of its best examples can be seen in Leckhampton Church, Holy Apostles Church, Cheltenham College Chapel and the Shire Hall at Gloucester. Hard limestones, known as Ragstones, were also exploited for later neo-Gothic buildings such as Francis Close Hall (now part of University of

Wagon Quarry, Leckhampton Hill, showing freestone (on face) and pea grit (on floor).

Gloucestershire) and for metalling roads and drystone walling. Apart from freestone, extracted from Postlip quarries to build Winchcombe Abbey and Winchcombe Church, Cleeve Hill quarries also yielded Pea Grit, used for many public buildings, including the plinth and weatherings of the Town Hall. Sands were also mined and transported by donkey to the Staffordshire potteries during the eighteenth and nineteenth centuries. Quarrying at Cleeve ceased in 1945 following concerns that the Iron Age hill fort and the common were being damaged.

Queen's Hotel

Built by architects Robert and Charles Jearrad in 1837–38 on the site of the Sherborne (later Imperial) Spa, the Queen's Hotel was the biggest hotel in Britain when it first opened. It was named in honour of Queen Victoria whose coronation occurred in 1838. Surprisingly, the hotel initially struggled to make money, and in 1852 it was sold for a paltry £8,400. However, this low price allowed extra investment to be made to restore, alter and improve the building. One of the enhancements made during the middle of the nineteenth century was to site a pair of Russian cannons captured at Sebastopol during the Crimean War on plinths in front of the hotel. These were later salvaged as scrap metal during the Second World War, and today only one of the plinths, now used as a flowerbed, remains. Famous guests have included General Sir Charles Napier, Edward VII when Prince of Wales, Adelina Patti, Sarah Bernhardt, Edward Elgar, Gordon Selfridge (of department store fame), Sir Arthur Conan Doyle, the explorer Fridtjof Nansen, Bob Hope (when it was used as an American Services Club during the Second World War), Prince Louis Jerome Napoleon and, in March 1990, the Prime Minister Mrs Thatcher and a number of Cabinet members.

The Russian cannons that were displayed in front of the hotel.

R

Regent Arcade

Built in 1982–84 on the site of the historic Plough Hotel, and opened in 1985, Cheltenham's 185,000-square-foot Regent Arcade is the town's largest shopping centre. The present-day building incorporates an approximate facsimile of the Plough's 1825 façade at its main entrance. Dating from at least 1654, The Plough was Cheltenham's leading hotel and coaching inn, comprising fifty-two bedrooms but just one bathroom. From here, fast stagecoaches such as *The Cheltenham Flyer* set out for London, arriving within 10.5 hours by 1826. Its extensive yard was reputed to be the largest in the country and could accommodate as many as sixty-two carriages. It was always viewed as the place 'to be seen'. The *English Spy* (1826) commented that 'if you wish to make a figure among the Chelts and be thought any thing of, you will, of course, domicile at the Plough'. Today, the arcade contains several interesting features, including the Wishing Fish Clock, 45 feet high, designed by artist and author Kit Williams, and built by Cheltenham

The Wishing Fish Clock.

clockmakers Sinclair Harding & Co. Unveiled in 1987, it is reputed to be the world's tallest mechanical clock. Another noteworthy item is a small commemorative model of a Gloster E28/39 jet recalling the time in 1940–41 when Frank Whittle designed Britain's first jet engine while working in the Regent Motors Garage, another building that predated the shopping centre on this site.

Robert Burns Avenue

Constructed as part of the Benhall Farm estate, Robert Burns Avenue should have been named after a Cotswold village in accordance with the estate's theme. However, the borough surveyor belatedly recalled a previous commitment to name it in 1959 to coincide with the bicentenary of the poet's birth. While poets such as Tennyson and Byron, through their strong associations with the town, had been previously commemorated in the street names of the St Mark's estate, Cheltenham's links with the descendants of Robert Burns (1759–96) had hitherto been overlooked. The poet's two sons, Lieutenant Colonel William Nicol Burns and Major James Glencairn Burns, had moved to Cheltenham in 1846 in retirement after military service in India, the latter remaining until his death in 1865. Both became well-known figures in local social circles. In the churchyard at St Mary's, Charlton Kings, stands an impressive memorial to the poet's granddaughters, Sarah and Annie Burns, and to his great-granddaughter, Margaret Constance Burns Hutchinson, who died between 1909 and 1925. It includes the last verse from Burns's prayer 'O Thou Dread Power' (1786): 'When, soon or late, they reach that coast, / O'er life's rough ocean driven, / May they rejoice, no wand'rer lost, / A family in Heaven!'

Memorial to descendants of Robert Burns (inset) in St Mary's churchyard, Charlton Kings.

S

Captain Henry Skillicorne

The life and achievements of the Manx-born sea captain Henry Skillicorne (1678–1763), regarded as the developer of Cheltenham as a spa resort, are summarised in what is reputedly the longest memorial in Britain. Comprising fifty-three lines and 593 words, his epitaph in St Mary's Church (now Cheltenham Minster) tells of his enterprise, following his retirement and then marriage to Elizabeth Mason, daughter of the owner of the land where the mineral springs had been discovered, 'to increase the knowledge, & extend the use of Cheltenham Spa'. A skilled linguist who could speak seven languages, Skillicorne had also travelled widely, trading in the Mediterranean,

Tour guide Phil Collins dressed as Captain Henry Skillicorne.

the Netherlands and America. Insights into his character are also given: 'He was of great Regularity & Probity, & so temperate as never to have been once intoxicated. Religious without Hypocrisy, Grave without Austerity, of a Cheerful Conversation without Levity, A kind Husband and tender Father. Tall, erect, robust, and active. From an Ill treated Wound while a Prisoner, after an Engagement at Sea, He became a strict Valetudinarian. He lived and dyed an honest man.' Curiously, the memorial should have been recorded slightly differently and been shortened by around 100 words had the instructions for the tablet, set out in the will of his son William who died in 1803, been fully carried out. One of the details, specified in William's will, but not included, was that his father 'died with the most beautiful set of Teeth, all sound, even and white as Ivory'! Today, his memory is further celebrated through a portrait bas-relief in the small garden behind the Town Hall and a fine oil painting acquired by The Wilson in 2015.

St George's Place

Reflecting its rise to become a leading evangelical stronghold during the nineteenth century, Cheltenham has many saints in its street names. However, one that probably originated from non-ecclesiastical sources was St George's Place. Originally known

King George III taking the waters at Cheltenham, by J. C. Stadler, 1812.

Sadler's Wells Puppet Theatre.

in the seventeenth century or earlier as Still's Lane and, for a short period, during the eighteenth century as Kent's Lane, its present name is thought to have been inspired by George III's visit of 1788. Eleven years later, a puppet theatre, Sadler's Wells, was established in former houses at Nos 67–69 St George's Place (now part of Chelsea Court flats). It was set up by Samuel Seward of Bristol, a talented actor and successful harlequin who previously worked at the London Sadler's Wells. Seward ran the theatre with his wife and two sons for nearly thirty years. One performance advertised in 1815 included displays of 'Slack Rope Vaulting', 'Posturing and Tumbling', an Italian Scaramouch, and 'an Enchanted Turk' who changed into six different figures! After Seward's death the theatre was reopened as the New Clarence Theatre in 1831, but was a short-lived success. The building later became Gardner's Academy, a private seminary, and then, in 1839, the Church of England Reading Association. Another building (now demolished) of historic interest was an old farmstead at No. 38 St George's Place. Dating from at least the 1740s, this was the home both of the Quaker William Mason, on whose land the first spa was discovered in 1716, and Captain Henry Skillicorne, who later developed it. The former puppet theatre buildings survived, recognised by few, until demolition in 2004.

Town Hall

Cheltenham's Edwardian baroque Town Hall was built on the site of a former bowling green in 1903 as the major venue for the town's cultural life, replacing the Assembly Rooms in the High Street, demolished in 1900. Soon after opening, its interior decoration drew some criticism, one reviewer asserting that 'the imitation marble pillars are suggestive of varnished corn beef and the yellow treatment of the capitals suggests that biliousness that would probably follow from a surfeit of corned beef varnished'. The main auditorium, which can accommodate around 900 seated guests, is particularly grand and includes balconies supported by Corinthian columns, and plaster-cast statues of Edward VII and George V, placed in niches on either side of the stage in 1916. The building also functioned for a time as the Central Spa. Opened in 1906, this venture was part of the Corporation's attempt to revive spa-going and promote Cheltenham as the 'Carlsbad of England'. To the left of the entrance hall is an octagonal counter with four Doulton ware urns for dispensing the water, only one of which now has a tap (non-functioning). Originally, it dispensed different types of mineral water. As the town's main venue for concerts and lectures the Town Hall has often hosted some of Cheltenham's most important historical events. It was here, for example, that

Town Hall.

T

Cheltenham's Antarctic explorer Dr Edward Wilson gave a memorable lecture in 1906 on the Discovery expedition (1901–04), six years before he perished with Captain Scott at the South Pole. More poignantly, in December 1912 Roald Amundsen gave a lecture about his successful polar conquest two months before the tragic news of the Scott/Wilson expedition reached Cheltenham. It was also here in 1927 that Gustav Holst conducted *The Planets* as part of a festival of his music organised by the local council.

Anthony Trollope

The writer Anthony Trollope (1815–82) visited Cheltenham from December 1852 to April 1853 while working as a post office surveyor. Staying at Paragon Buildings (now Nos 126–36 Bath Road), he later modelled No. 7 Paragon, the heroine's lodgings in *Miss Mackenzie* (1865) where 'every house … looks out upon the Montpelier [*sic*] Gardens', on his own lodgings. Known for his satirical writing, Trollope regularly poked fun at Cheltenham, sometimes portraying it in his novels as Littlebath. It is thought that his dislike for Cheltenham arose during the early 1830s when his father's plans to become a gentleman farmer were thwarted by John Rushout, 2nd Baron Northwick. As a powerful property developer who was active in Cheltenham, acquiring Thirlestaine House in 1838 to house his nationally important collection of 1,500 old master paintings, Northwick was described by Anthony Trollope as a 'cormorant who was eating us up'. On one occasion Trollope even helped his father flee to Belgium so that he could avoid paying his debts to Northwick.

Paragon Buildings, where Anthony Trollope lived.

Revd Francis Close.

Another cause for Trollope's dislike for the town is revealed in *The Bertrams* (1859) where, we are told, that the pious women in Littlebath, 'never cease ... making slippers for their clergymen'. This significant detail links directly to Revd Francis Close, whose dominance in the town led Tennyson to dub him the town's 'Pope'. Such was his appeal to his congregation that, during the thirty-year period (1826–56) he served as rector, Close received around 1,500 pairs of slippers from his followers! Trollope's contempt for Close arose from his experience as a post office surveyor when he was trying to introduce postal deliveries on a Sunday. His attempts were opposed by Close, a strict Sabbatarian once hailed as the Church of England cleric who achieved the best observance of the Sabbath outside Scotland. Not only did he persuade 500 shopkeepers not to open on Sunday but also ensured that only two mail trains stopped at Cheltenham station on Sunday for six years after the Birmingham and Bristol railway was built through Cheltenham in 1840.

After Close succeeded in thwarting Trollope's proposals, the novelist took his revenge through his pen. In *Barchester Towers* (1857), for example, it is thought that Obadiah Slope, the self-promoting, manipulating and sycophantic curate who preaches against 'Sabbath travelling', is modelled on Close. In *Miss Mackenzie*, Close is depicted as Mr Stumfold who 'was always fighting the devil by opposing those pursuits which are the life and mainstay of such places as Littlebath'. These included playing cards, dancing, horse-racing, and hunting, all of which were vehemently opposed by Close in real life. Significantly, there was also a 'Stumfoldian edict ... ordaining that no Stumfoldian in Littlebath should be allowed to receive a letter on Sundays'.

Tuckwell Theatre

Perhaps the town's most secluded building is the Tuckwell Theatre. Located in a hidden corner of Dean Close School, since 2003 it has hosted Cheltenham's annual summer Open-air Theatre Festival. Ironically, the theatre belongs to an institution dedicated to the memory of the evangelical rector Francis Close (1797–82). Known for his vehement opposition to drama and the theatre, Close claimed that the art form had 'proved itself to be a matter of immorality and vice' and, in 1850, declared that those who frequent the theatre are 'criminally answerable for all the consequences'. When Cheltenham's Theatre Royal burned down in 1839, fingers pointed accusingly in Close's direction. Unsurprisingly, therefore, it took the school some time to dispel its puritanical distrust of theatre. The person who helped to change the school's views was C. A. P. Tuckwell, an English and Drama schoolmaster who joined the staff in 1923. When he joined, outdoor school plays were presented in the Headmaster's garden, but Tuckwell soon promoted the idea of a purpose-built outdoor theatre.

The theatre's construction, largely achieved through the combined efforts of the masters and boys, began in 1934. Expert advice on the tiered arena was provided by the architect Sir Philip Stott, famous locally for his restoration of Stanton village. Stott also donated 500 interlinking concrete blocks, which today still form the tiered seats. On 12 June 1937, the new theatre was opened by the Shakespearean actor Randle Ayrton, who read some dedicatory lines penned for the occasion by the Poet Laureate John Masefield. Its first production was *King John*. Since then the theatre has risen to the panoply of challenges affecting an outdoor performing arts space. A routine was soon put in place, for example, requesting local residents in nearby gardens to cease cutting lawns or lighting bonfires during performances and, when necessary, profuse quantities of insect repellent were made available to improve audiences' comfort on warm summer evenings. During the blackout years of the Second World War, evening performances were switched to the afternoon. Fortunately, the sound of passing aircraft landing and taking off from nearby Staverton Airport has never presented major problems, while the gentle trickle from the adjacent Hatherley Brook accompanied by pleasant birdsong have only contributed to the special atmosphere of this unique venue.

The Tuckwell Theatre, Cheltenham's hidden outdoor theatre.

U

UCAS

A familiar name to anyone applying for higher education courses, UCAS (Universities and Colleges Admissions Service) has been in Cheltenham for over fifty years. Formed in London in 1961 with a team of twenty-five when it was known as UCCA (Universities Central Council on Admissions), the organisation's original remit was to help universities effectively manage multiple applications from students in England and Wales. In 1968, UCCA moved to Rodney House in Rodney Road, bringing twenty-nine of its eighty-two staff from London. In 1989, it moved again, to Fulton House (Jessop Avenue), and merged with its partner organisations PCAS (Polytechnics Central Admissions System) and SCUE (Standing Conference on University Entrance) to form UCAS, as an independent admissions organisation. Today, UCAS's current headquarters, opened by Princess Anne in September 1999, are located at Rosehill (opposite Cheltenham racecourse). Previously, this site was occupied by a house, also called Rosehill, built in 1824–25 within 8.5-acre grounds. Designed by the

UCAS's current headquarters at Rosehill.

U

architect John Buonarotti Papworth, who is recognised for setting the blueprint for the typical Cheltenham villa at Regent House (Montpellier Parade) and for adding the fine Rotunda to enhance the Montpellier Spa, Rosehill was originally built for a Bath doctor, John Shoolbred. It was extensively remodelled *c.* 1870 in a distinctive Franco-Italianate style, and renamed Prestbury Park, which functioned as a residential hotel in 1935–50. Unfortunately, the house was demolished in 1993 to make way for the construction of Gulf Oil's headquarters, the site reverting to the Rosehill name. In 1997, Gulf Oil moved out of the building. Now employing over 450 members of staff, UCAS processes more than 3 million undergraduate applications every year.

George Allen Underwood

Despite his short life, the Bath-born architect George Allen Underwood (1793–1829) made a considerable contribution to Cheltenham's townscape. Following his training at the London office of Sir John Soane from 1807 to 1815, he established his own practice in Cheltenham. Here, he was responsible for designing the Montpellier Spa (1817) with a Doric colonnade, its dome being added later by J. B. Papworth; Sherborne or Imperial Spa (1818), replaced by the Queen's Hotel; the Masonic Hall (1820–1823), outside London, the world's first purpose-built Masonic hall and Cheltenham's oldest non-ecclesiastical public building still used for its original purpose; Holy Trinity Church (1820–1823), built in a Gothic style; and the façade of the Plough Hotel (*c.* 1826, demolished 1982 to build the Regent Arcade).

Montpellier Spa, by Henry Lamb (1823), six years after it was opened.

V

Vittoria Walk

The road was named sometime after Wellington's 1813 Peninsular War victory in Spain, following the renaming of Hygeia House, its first principal building, as Vittoria House. In 1804 it was the residence of the Liverpool and London banker Henry Thompson. It was here, prior to the success of his Montpellier Spa in 1809, that Thompson was able to dispense medicinal water after piping it from various boreholes sunk nearby. The road also once housed perhaps Cheltenham's most idiosyncratic building. This was the Rock House, originally dating from 1815, when it was known as Waterloo Cottage, but from 1842 remodelled to resemble a grotto turned inside out. Its façade was clad with dark and lighter-coloured rock, and conches, while its interior, thought to have been constructed from the ballast of Captain Hardy's ship, incorporated stalactites 'growing down' from the roof and coral and fossilised creatures embedded in curved rock-faced walls. Sadly, this unique building was demolished in 1978.

Vittoria House (formerly Hygeia House, home of Henry Thompson).

Hugo van Wadenoyen

One of the town's eccentric characters was the photographer Hugo van Wadenoyen (1892–1959) whose studio was located at No. 79 Promenade in 1936–56. Of Dutch descent, he settled in Cheltenham in the early 1930s. At first, he was viewed with some suspicion on account of his association with the Tolstoyan Whiteway Colony near Stroud, run on utopian socialist ideology, and where he lived in a converted Caledonian Railway carriage. Despite this, he quickly established a reputation for high-quality artistic photography, excelling particularly in informal portraits of children, which were in stark contrast to the prevailing formal approaches. At 6 feet tall and bald, with a camera always around his neck, his lean and slightly stooped frame made him a well-known figure along The Promenade. Those who knew him remembered him standing out from the crowds, whether with his prominent nose or with a cigarette resting on the corner of his mouth, peering left and right through large horn-rimmed spectacles. However, his influence was far from parochial. An avid promoter of photography as an art form, he conveyed pioneering ideas about portraiture and landscape photography through frequent lectures,

Self-portrait, by Hugo van Wadenoyen.

radio broadcasts and books, among which *Photographing People: Ways to New Portraiture* (1939) and *Wayside Snapshots* (1947) were seminal works. One of his most influential ideas was to reject pictorialism in landscape photography, advocating direct realism instead of the prevailing approach of making photographs look like engravings. Although sometimes regarded as a loner, Hugo counted the artist, John Piper, as one of his close friends who regularly came to visit him in Cheltenham. Also, among his many admirers was John Betjeman, who once wrote to Cecil Beaton to say that Hugo was very much 'my type [of photographer]'. Examples of his local work can be seen at the Local and Family History Centre as well as The Wilson, where there is a portrait of him by Rhoda Elliott.

Well Place

Although Cheltenham's most famous wells were located mainly in the Bayshill, Montpellier, Cambray and Pittville areas, some were also opened in the Lansdown and Christchurch districts. Well Place, for example, located between Christchurch Road and Douro Road, derives from the Chadnor Villa Well, a small saline well run by Miss Ann Webb from 1857. It was one of several wells in the area whose waters fed the collecting tank of a Pumper's Cottage in Christ Church Road. From here the waters were pumped around 1 mile through lead pipes to Montpellier Pump Room, where different taps dispensed different varieties of water, and then on down the hill to Montpellier Baths, now The Playhouse. Here it was used to produce Real Cheltenham Salts in the adjoining manufactory.

The Pumper's Cottage from where water was pumped to Montpellier.

Statue of William IV.

William IV

Cheltenham's statue of William IV is one of only three in existence, the others located at Greenwich and Göttingen, one of Cheltenham's twin towns. It depicts the king in robes and was erected to mark his coronation in 1831. Originally sited in Imperial Gardens, it was moved to Montpellier Gardens in 1920.

Dr Edward Wilson

One of Cheltenham's most famous sons, Edward Adrian Wilson was born in 1872 at No. 6 (now No. 91) Montpellier Terrace. A doctor, naturalist, artist and leading member of Captain Scott's Discovery (1901–04) and Terra Nova (1910–12) expeditions, he undertook important scientific work and was perhaps the last great practitioner of exploration art. He was one of five men who reached the South Pole on 17 January 1912, only to discover that the Norwegian Roald Amundsen had arrived there five weeks earlier. During the return journey, Edgar Evans and Lawrence Oates fell ill and died; and later, around 29 March, Wilson, Henry 'Birdie' Bowers and Scott perished in their blizzard-blown tent, only 11 miles from their next food depot.

Statue of Dr Edward Wilson created by Lady Scott.

In 1874 the Wilson family moved to a ten-bedroom detached Regency villa called Westal (demolished, site now occupied by Eagle Tower car park) in Montpellier Parade which later, in 1907, was the venue for an important meeting with Ernest Shackleton. In 1886–91 Wilson attended Cheltenham College as a day pupil. This allowed him the freedom to explore the countryside around The Crippetts, a farm his family rented at the top of Crippetts Lane. It was here, a place he described as 'a little piece of heaven', where he developed his skills in art and natural history. He never forgot his love for Cheltenham, returning frequently to visit his family and friends, and to give lectures at Cheltenham College and the Town Hall. After Cheltenham received news of the tragedy at the South Pole in 1913, a plan was formed to hang a pair of commemorative medallions to Wilson and Scott in the Town Hall. However, his widow Oriana objected, preferring an open-air memorial instead since her husband 'was such a lover of nature, and at all times avoided being in buildings as much as possible'. A statue of him was created by Lady Scott (Scott's widow) and unveiled in front of a large crowd on the Promenade on 9 July 1914. In 1924 a memorial window to Wilson was installed at Cheltenham College representing the Christian virtue of Fortitude. Today his name is also recalled through Edward Wilson House, a four-storey block of flats on Princess Elizabeth Way, and the art gallery and museum which, in 2013, was renamed The Wilson after Edward Adrian and his father Edward Thomas Wilson, one of the town's great worthies.

Winter Garden

Dubbed 'Cheltenham's Crystal Palace', the Winter Garden was built in 1878 at a cost of £30,000 in Imperial Gardens to a design by local architect John Thomas Darby. With brick walls and an iron and glass roof, culminating in a dome nearly 100 feet high, it could accommodate 2,000 people and was originally intended to be used for concerts, exhibitions and bazaars. However, one of its earliest successes proved to be a roller-skating rink, one of the first in the country which, according to the *Cheltenham Looker-On*, formed 'the preferable attraction, enlivened as it was by a Band of seven instruments, whose performances ... were effectually marred by the ceaseless clatter of the roller skates'. Despite this success, there were frequent changes of ownership, and in 1895 the building was bought by the council. Thereafter, it was also used for auctions, circuses and as a repertory theatre and cinema. In 1916 it became a shadow factory where Bristol Fighter Aircraft were made. By the time the Second World War came its days were numbered. Although it dwarfed the neighbouring Town Hall, many of the entertainments transferred to the latter which provided efficient heating and better acoustics. Despite its demolition in 1940, there are clues to its former existence in the layout of the paths in the ornamental gardens, which align with the position of the garden's entrances.

Winter Garden.

X

(E)xmouth Arms

One of the oldest pubs in the town, possibly dating from before 1820, the Exmouth Arms in Bath Road was named after the prominent naval admiral Sir Edward Pellew (1757–1833), who became Viscount Exmouth following his heroic victory at the Bombardment of Algiers in 1816, which secured the release of 1,200 Christian slaves. Afterwards, he was widely fêted and, on 24 October, arrived in Cheltenham in grand fashion. *The Morning Post* reported that his carriage was drawn from the town entrance at London Road to his lodgings in Royal Crescent by a party of men wearing blue ribbons, preceded by a cheering crowd and military band playing 'See, the Conqu'ring Hero Comes'. Over the years, the Exmouth Arms site has provided a number of additional facilities and services. During the 1820s, for example, an outdoor swimming pool known as Parker's Swimming and Bathing Place was located behind the west end of the present beer garden, fed by the confluence of the Nolty and Westal Brooks. Later, it was converted into a bowling ground, where skittles and quoits were also played. Additionally, in keeping with common practices during the nineteenth century, the Exmouth Arms was occasionally used for hearing coroner's inquests. Examples of cases included a 'temporary insanity' verdict returned for a man found drowned in 1851 in a pond 50 yards from his home in Naunton Crescent, and 'accidental poisoning' for a seven-week old daughter, living in St Philips Street, who was given laudanum instead of rhubarb syrup by her mother after her elder child passed her the wrong bottle from a high shelf.

Exmouth Arms.

Y

York Passage

One of the most interesting examples of the courts and passages that radiate off the High Street, York Passage (now part of Grosvenor Terrace), was named after the adjacent York Hotel, one of the principal inns in the coaching era, where members of the exiled French royal family stayed in 1811. In 1782 it housed Cheltenham's first purpose-built theatre, which witnessed performances by several famous actresses, including Sarah Siddons (1755–1831) and Harriet Mellon (1777–1837) who later married the rich banker Thomas Coutts and subsequently became the Duchess of St Albans. During George III's visit in July 1788 the royal party attended the theatre (allowing it to be renamed the Theatre Royal) to see Dorothy Jordan (1761–1816), who later became the future William IV's mistress, perform Rosalind in *As You Like It*.

Sarah Siddons, who performed on several occasions in Cheltenham.

Z

Zeppelin

'Zeppelin' was the original name of a house at No. 19 Priors Road. Built *c.* 1900 the house was named after the German Count Ferdinand von Zeppelin, who pioneered the development of rigid airships. The name of the neighbouring house at No. 21, formerly known as Dumont, was also inspired by a pioneer of dirigibles, the Brazilian Alberto Santos-Dumont. The house names were probably discontinued promptly, following the use of Zeppelins during the First World War for reconnaissance and bombing raids. Although Cheltenham never received any Zeppelin attacks, as they were confined to the east coast, enforcement of a blackout in 1916 helped to reduce the perceived risk. It was as late as 3 July 1932 that Cheltenham witnessed its first airship, the entire population thrilled to watch the Graf Zeppelin cruising over the town as part of the airship's tour of the British Isles. During the 1930s the Graf Zeppelin provided regular transatlantic flights from Germany to North America and Brazil.

The Graf Zeppelin near Southam, 3 July 1932.

Zona Works

Located in Russell Place (between Swindon Road and Tewkesbury Road), on the site now occupied by Wickes, was the Zona Works factory. In 1922 this was the newly built home of Messrs W. H. Cole and Co., Ltd (established in 1867) who manufactured high-grade hair pins. By 1938 they were producing the pins at a rate of 100 per minute and had diversified their product range to include aircraft fittings and fashion accessories such as hair grips and dress hooks and eyes. In 1945, Zona Works was bought by Delapena and Sons Ltd, specialists in honing equipment. The company was credited with helping to secure the Allies' victory during the Second World War at the Battle of Alamein, where their honing equipment was used to repair faulty gun barrels prior to their deployment. W. H. Cole, under Delapena's ownership, then produced a wide range of honing equipment, primarily as export for the automotive, and aviation industries, and for honing glass hydraulic syringes. By 1950 the company, by then also producing garage equipment and radio frequency heating equipment, had a workforce of 250 and became one of the first to successfully apply radio frequency heating technology in the post-war industrial field.

In 1946, the firm also showed their ability to innovate when the works director invented a toy pedal car that could be converted into a push chair.

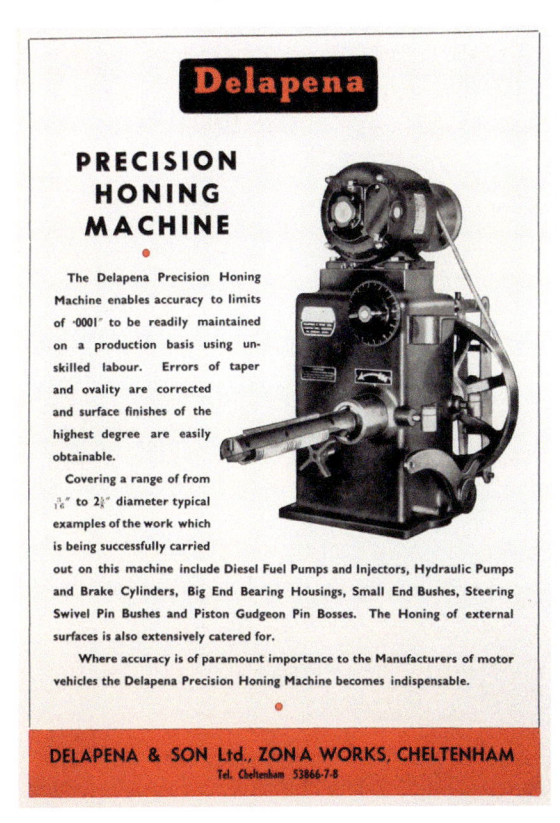

Advertisement from Graces Guide, 1948.

Zoological Gardens

During the 1830s Cheltenham was at the centre of two ambitious, but rival, schemes to establish a zoological garden in the town. From around 1834 Thomas Billings, a local solicitor who purchased the 20-acre Park Estate in 1831, planned to site the Gloucestershire Zoological, Botanical and Horticultural Gardens in the centre of his estate. However, from 1836 another scheme run by speculators favouring the northern side of town sought to develop the Cheltenham Zoological Garden on a 16-acre site in a field to the east of Pittville Pump Room. Today the area covers the environs of Cakebridge Road and part of Pittville School. This planned to accommodate a range of animals, including zebras, kangaroos, rhinoceros, camels, elephants, alligators, monkeys, and pelicans. The Gloucestershire Zoological, Botanical and Horticultural Gardens opened briefly from 28 June 1838 on The Park estate before being redeveloped as public pleasure grounds. This zoo comprised a small aviary and museum housed in its Italian-style entrance lodge (once existing near the present Fullwood Lodge), which included cockatoo, Java sparrows and a collection of stuffed hummingbirds. Elsewhere, it contained some rare waterfowl, stork, spoonbill, a Brahman bull and small mammals such as monkeys and otter. The Pittville scheme never got off the drawing board, and a mixture of in-fighting between the rival approaches and the lack of firm financial backing proved decisive. Today the attractively laid out grounds in The Park, now owned by the University of Gloucestershire, still provide tangible reminders of its short-lived history as a zoo, both in its ornamental lake designed in the shape of Africa (another was planned in the shape of the Americas), and in the main walkway known as Elephant Walk.

Elephant Walk, The Park.

Select Bibliography

Blake, Steven and Beacham, Roger, *The Book of Cheltenham* (London: Barracuda Books, 1982)

Bradbury, Oliver, *Cheltenham's Lost Heritage* (Stroud: Sutton Publishing, 2004)

The British Newspaper Archive, *www.britishnewspaperarchive.co.uk*

Brooks, Robin, *The Story of Cheltenham* (Stroud: Sutton Publishing, 2003)

Chatwin, Amina, *Cheltenham's Ornamental Ironwork* (Cheltenham: Amina Chatwin, 1975)

'Cheltonia: the Curiosities of Cheltenham Spa, Past and Present', *https://cheltonia.wordpress.com/*

Cheltenham Local History Society, journals and other publications, *www.cheltlocalhistory.org.uk*

Elder, David, *Cheltenham Heritage Walks* (Stroud: Amberley Publishing, 2014)

Elder, David, *Cheltenham in 50 Buildings* (Stroud: Amberley Publishing, 2017)

Elder, David, *Secret Cheltenham* (Stroud: Amberley Publishing, 2019)

Goding, John, *Norman's History of Cheltenham* (Cheltenham: Norman, 1863)

Hart, Gwen, *A History of Cheltenham* (Leicester: Leicester University Press, 1965)

Hodsdon, James, *An Historical Gazetteer of Cheltenham* (Stroud: Bristol and Gloucestershire Archaeological Society, 1997)

Jones, Anthea, *Cheltenham: A New History* (Lancaster: Carnegie Publishing, 2010)

Rowbotham, Sue and Waller, Jill, *Cheltenham: A History* (Chichester, Phillimore, 2004)

Sampson, Aylwin and Blake, Steven, *A Cheltenham Companion* (Cheltenham: Portico Press, 1993)

Acknowledgements

I am most grateful to Alan Murphy at Amberley for commissioning this book. Also, a number of museums, libraries and archive services have provided me with excellent support. My thanks in particular go to all the staff at Cheltenham Local Studies Centre. I am most grateful to a number of individuals who have commented on drafts, contributed material or arranged for me to visit specific buildings. Particular thanks go to Dr Steven Blake, Dr James Hodsdon, Catherine Howe, Martin Hughes, Laura Kinnear, Brian McGurk, Rachael Merrison, Eric and Margaret Miller, Paul Milton, Nick Norman, Christopher Rainey, Rachel Roberts, Julie Sargent, Jessica Shapiro, Anne Strathie, Grace Pritchard Woods, Craig Walker and Carol Wright. I am also grateful to the following: David Hollier for permission to publish my image of his artwork on p.9; and Camilla Meeuwissen-True for information about UCAS and the accompanying image on p.82.

I am also grateful to the following for copyright permission to use various images: GCHQ Press Office for images on p.31; Cheltenham Local Studies Centre for the historic photographs, prints and drawings on p.18, p.22 (left), p.23, p.34, p.52, p.59, p.61, and p.83; Jill Waller for the images on p.28 and p.86; Neela Mann for the images on p.11, p.20, p.46, p.58 p.68 and p.89; Julie Sargent for the image on p.48; Lloyds Bank for the image on p.53; Conway Hall Ethical Society for the portrait of George Jacob Holyoake (1817–1906) on p.37 by Holyoake's nephew Rowland Holyoake, 1902; the Mitchell Library, State Library of New South Wales for the image on p.77 (from *Watercolour drawings of theatres and other buildings in towns of the south of England: the original drawings for James Winston's Theatric Tourist, 1805*, 1802) courtesy of the Theatres Trust www.theatrestrust.org.uk; David Hanks for the images on p.6 and p.13; Wellcome Collection for images on p.41 and p.76; Phil Collins for the image on p.75; Dr Robert Billings for the image on p.10; John Redfern and Ally McConnell of the Dowty Heritage project for the images on p.24 (left inset and right); Cheltenham College Archives for the image on p.33; Sue Rowbotham for the image on p.69 (above); Cheltenham Camera Club Archives for the image on p.85; and Geoff North for the image on p.92. The images on p.8 and p.91 are reproduced from the collections of the Library of Congress. The copyright of all other images belongs to the author. Finally, my heartfelt thanks go to my family, Meg, Rachel, and Catrin, for their patience, support and encouragement.